IMAGES
of America

WASHINGTON, D.C.
A HISTORICAL WALKING TOUR

A Tour Vehicle Operating in Washington, D.C. in the Late 19th Century.

IMAGES
of America

WASHINGTON, D.C.
A HISTORICAL WALKING TOUR

Thomas J. Carrier

ARCADIA

First published 1999
Reprinted 2000, 2001, 2002, 2003, 2004, 2005

Published by Arcadia Publishing
Charleston SC, Chicago IL, Portsmouth NH, San Francisco CA

Printed in Great Britain

Library of Congress Catalog Card Number: 99-62491

For all general information contact Arcadia Publishing at:
Telephone 843-853-2070
Fax 843-853-0044
E-mail sales@arcadiapublishing.com
For customer service and orders:
Toll-Free 1-888-313-2665

Visit us on the internet at http://www.arcadiapublishing.com

"CAPTURE OF THE CITY OF WASHINGTON." This image depicts the burning of Washington, D.C. on the night of August 24, 1814, by 4,500 British soldiers. (Photo courtesy of Washingtoniana Division, D.C. Public Library.)

CONTENTS

ACKNOWLEDGMENTS

Without the special support of the following, this book could never have been published:

James M. Goode, whose books *Capitol Losses* and *The Outdoor Sculpture of Washington D.C.* are the inspirations behind these tours and are themselves historical pieces; Natalie and Edward Hughes of the Bookhouse in Arlington, Virginia, who allowed me complete access to their extensive American history collection as if it were my personal library; Mary Tiernes and Matthew Gilmore of the Washingtoniana Division of the Martin Luther King Public Library, whose extensive collection and incredible patience helped make this book a reality; Don Hawkins, chairman of Parks and History Association, and Phil Ogilvie, chairman of the editorial board of the Historical Society of Washington, for their infectious confidence early on; Keith Melder, chairman emeritus of the Division of Social History of the National Museum of American History, for editing the final draft for historical accuracy, still, any and all errors are my own; Heather Moore of the Historical Office of the United States Senate for her spirited enthusiasm; Al Eisenberg for the use of some key Civil War-era photographs from his private collection; and Gail Redmond, librarian of the Historical Society of Washington, D.C., for her professional help.

Special dedications reserved for the following:

Arlene Bournia, whose special support will always be why I can put my thoughts into action. Christine Riley, my editor at Arcadia Publishing, for her great patience and continuous support. Renee del Solar for her bright and cheerful support and for the use of her camera for "one week." To my Inés, my wonderful wife, who continues to amaze me with her loving support, encouragement, and boundless love. To Pat Donofrio, who would have been proud, and most importantly, to my Ma and Dad, who keep me grounded.

About the author: Thomas J. Carrier has been a licensed tour guide in Washington, D.C. since 1995, although he has given unofficial tours since he visited the area while stationed at Fort Bragg, North Carolina, in the late 1970s. He has also written *The Historic Walking Tour of Alexandria 1749*. He has given specialized tours to the curator and the Secret Service at the White House and was a costumed interpreter for the National Park Service. He is now a conference planning consultant in Washington, D.C.

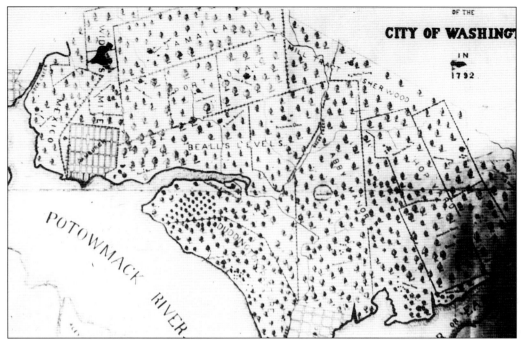

WASHINGTON, D.C. MAP OF 1792.

The Federal City: From Farmland to World Capital

The first human settlement in the area of what is now Washington, D.C., was around the year 1600 in the Native American town of Nacotchtant near the Anacostia River. In 1608, Capt. John Smith may have traveled past Washington, D.C., down to Little Falls, although that distinction is still in dispute by historians. Throughout the 17th century, the area was owned and managed under the land grant system with estates of 1,000 acres or more being distributed by the monarch in England. The proprietors of these estates, known as manors, were lords. Each manor was its own town with tobacco, the chief money-making and trading crop, and slavery, providing cheap labor for general production.

Because hotels, aside from small taverns and inns, were unknown, the social scene of the area consisted of hospitality provided by the manors. Each manor provided overnight accommodations for travelers and "any decent stranger." It was customary to provide overnight lodgings and a meal to any passer-by. This reasoning assumed that when someone from the manor traveled, the favor would be returned. George Washington recorded that his family did not sit down to dinner alone for 20 years. Card parties, horse races, fencing, sports, shooting matches, and other outdoor activities occupied each family and manor throughout its "proper season."

The two important regional trading centers were located at Saw Pit Landing, known as Georgetown since its organization in 1751, and at Hunting Creek Warehouse, also known as Belle Haven but organized in 1749 as Alexandria. The proximity of these two important seaports provided more justification for the location of the new Federal City nearby.

When the Constitution was passed in 1789, setting out the boundaries of the new capital and

7

a new government, the area now known as Washington, D.C., consisted largely of farmlands held by 19 families. These properties, split from original land grants, had been changing hands through inheritance or sale (usually within the same small circle of people, with many related by marriage) for nearly 100 years. They all knew each other and shared the bonds of civic office, militia service, and church responsibilities as their duty. The terms by which private lands were to be purchased by the federal government for parks, public buildings, and streets and alleys were laid out by George Washington in his March 31, 1791 letter to Thomas Jefferson:

All the land from Rock-creek along the river to the eastern-branch and so upward to or above the ferry including a breadth of about a mile and a half the whole containing from three to five thousand acres is ceded to the public on condition that when the whole shall be surveyed and laid off as a city [which Major L'Enfant is now directed to do] the present Proprietors shall retain every other lot; and for such of the land as may be taken for public use, for squares, walks, &ca, they be allowed at the rate of Twenty-five pounds per acre—The Public having the right to reserve such parts of the wood on the land as may be thought necessary to be preserved for ornament &ca. The Landholder to have the use and profits of all their ground until the city is laid off into lots and sale is made of those lots which by the agreement become public property. No compensation is to be made for the ground that may be occupied as streets or alleys.

In 1790, the new site for the Federal City—George Washington didn't like to refer to it as the City of Washington—covered about 5,000 acres of hills and valleys, nearly the size of the city of London. According to legend, it was dominated by marshland, not swampland, on the south pasture, now the area known as the Mall. Also included were farms near the White House and Capitol areas and undeveloped woods throughout. The total population, between 3,000 and 5,000, was situated mostly in and around Georgetown, an important regional tobacco port.

By 1800, the population had grown to 14,093, and by 1820, it was 33,039. Yet, the area only began losing its "backwoods" reputation after the massive construction of streets, sewer lines, and parks by Alexander "Boss" Shepard in the 1870s. From then on, the "City of Magnificent Distances" steadily grew to become a world capital known for its art, theatre, inventions, landmarks, history, and, of course, for its politics.

L'ENFANT'S PLAN FOR WASHINGTON, D.C., 1800.

The best way to tell the story of early Washington, D.C., is through someone who has lived it. Christian Hines was nine years old when construction on the new capital city began in 1791. He was born in Georgetown in 1781, when it was part of Frederick County, Maryland. He died in 1875 at the age of 94 and hardly ever left Washington, D.C. In 1866, he dictated an oral history providing a detailed account of where every building, house, and government building was located in early Washington, D.C. He had met every president from Washington through Grant and remembered helping Pres. John Quincy Adams put out a fire in the Treasury Building as part of a "bucket brigade." Other reminiscences are scattered throughout as many sites as possible.

ALEXANDER "BOSS" SHEPARD.

As you walk through the neighborhoods and visit memorials, official buildings, and private homes, you are missing so much more than this limited format can provide. At each site, tried to show what was there before the current structure existed. Due to limited resources, however, I can't always succeed. As you visit a site that welcomes visitors, remember that each historic site may emphasize certain parts of their history over others. Don't be afraid to ask questions. You are expected to. To explore the history of Washington, D.C., in depth, begin with the selected bibliography on page 127 of this book. Also, remember to look up as you are walking. You might discover something old that is new to you.

What was once considered a hazardous duty for a foreign diplomat, Washington, D.C., is now considered a preeminent posting and a significant boost to an international career. The extraordinary diversity of Washington, D.C., is not limited to its people, but also can be found in its architectural and historical heritage. Enjoy your tour. Perhaps you will make history here, too.

WASHINGTON, D.C., IN 1862.

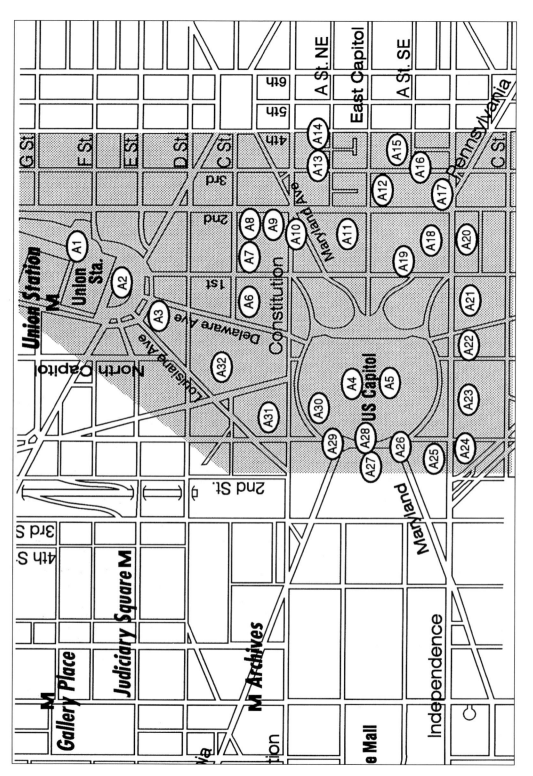

Tour A

CAPITOL HILL

> *". . . I could not discover one in all respects so advantageous*
> *. . . as a pedestal waiting for a superstructure . . ."*
>
> —*Pierre L'Enfant in a letter to George Washington*

The original patent for what eventually would become Capitol Hill was granted to George Thompson. These 1,800 acres were granted as the first patent in the area by Lord Baltimore in 1663. The land eventually became part of Charles Carroll's holdings in the late 17th century after he arrived in Maryland as the newly appointed attorney general of the Maryland colony by Lord Baltimore in 1680.

Daniel Carroll of Duddington, Charles's second son, became the second generation Carroll to own the site that is now Capitol Hill. He acquired the 500-acre estate, known then as Jenkins Hill (it is unclear where the name originated), from his father. In 1791, the area was renamed Federal Hill by Pierre L'Enfant in a letter to President Washington, where it was described as "a pedestal waiting for a superstructure."

Until the Civil War, residential and commercial development in this area remained slow because of absurdly high land prices. Like so many others, even George Washington lost his original investment on his twin townhouses built near the Capitol.

Only in the latter part of the 20th century, after many years of decline, has Capitol Hill undergone a transformation. It is now an active center of national life for Congress and the Supreme Court. Private homes built before the Civil War are few, but Capitol Hill's collection of post–Civil War architecture is returning to its original promise of a great neighborhood.

SITE A1: UNION STATION. During the last half of the 19th century, two separate and inconvenient train terminals existed. Their tracks and steam engine locomotives literally ran down the middle of city streets and across the Mall. The confusion, noise, general shabbiness, and, most importantly, safety hazards all contributed to a persistent cry for a unified railroad terminal. The famous McMillan Plan of 1901 went beyond planning a train terminal to also include significant changes to L'Enfant's original plan for the Federal City. Union Station was approved, and architect Daniel Burnham's Roman classic design was completed in 1907. The above photo shows what is now North Capitol Park, *c.* 1920. By 1976, the station was converted into the National Visitors Center, but closed shortly thereafter and remained vacant. Beginning in 1981, Union Station was developed into commercial property and reopened to great fanfare in 1988.

UNION STATION ACCIDENT. Inherent in any railroad station is the possibility of a train completing its run inside the station itself, as did this Pennsylvania Railroad engine on January 16, 1953. Its brakes failed, and it sailed past the tracks right into the Union Station concourse. No one was killed. In this original photo from the *Washington Star* newspaper, the train was already lowered from its initial impact site to enable it to be turned on its side. After the train was below floor level, a temporary floor was built above the wreckage until after the inauguration of President Dwight D. Eisenhower on January 20.

SITE A2: COLUMBUS FOUNTAIN. From behind, you will notice a 3-foot-tall medallion in bas relief showing King Ferdinand and Queen Isabella of Spain, who sponsored Columbus's expeditions. The center of this marble memorial is a 45-foot shaft topped by a large globe with the outline of the Western Hemisphere carved in relief. Sculptor Loredo Taft created a 15-foot statue of Columbus. From the base is the prow of a ship with a figurehead symbolizing Discovery. On the right side, facing Columbus, is an elderly figure representing the Old World; on the left is the figure of an American Indian symbolizing the New World. The three flagpoles just behind the fountain represent the *Nina*, the *Pinta*, and the *Santa Maria*, the ships bearing Columbus to the New World in 1492. The entire fountain was installed in 1912.

SITE A3: NORTH CAPITOL PARK. Close to Union Station stood several significant buildings dating to Washington's earliest history. The photo shows the Union Plaza Dormitories (at bottom), consisting of 18 temporary Colonial Revival-style dormitories located directly in front of Union Station. These dormitories housed 2,000 women during World War I. The buildings were intended to alleviate the serious overcrowding in Washington and were reserved only for government workers. After the war, they continued to be used as government offices. An earlier building on this site included the Fire Truck Company No. 1 D.C. Fire Department. The company moved to its firehouse here in 1879 and renamed Truck Company No. 1 in 1906. To the right of the park fountains stood George Washington's Townhouses (see bronze marker), two attached townhouses built by Washington in 1798 to entice developers to the area. All of these structures were razed to complete North Capitol Park in 1930.

THE CAPITOL AFTER BEING BURNED BY BRITISH FORCES, AUGUST 24, 1814. The British troops under Major General Robert Ross and Rear Admiral George Cockburn and his force of about 150 regulars entered the city on August 24, 1814 and immediately burned the Capitol and then continued up Pennsylvania Avenue to burn the White House as well. The raid ended only when thunderstorms rolled in toward evening.

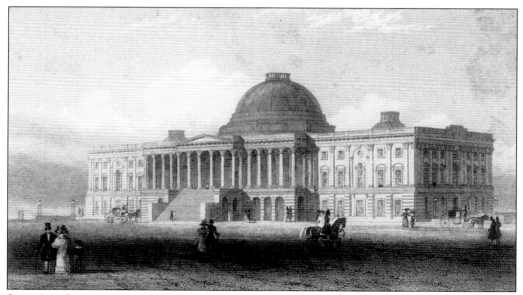

SITE A4: CAPITOL WITH WOODEN DOME BY CHARLES BULFINCH, 1825–1865. Where you are standing is near the original part of the Capitol where the first Congress convened in November 1800. It was a spot chosen specifically by Pierre L'Enfant and approved by George Washington because, at 88 feet above the Potomac, it afforded a commanding view of the Federal City. Beginning with only a boxy senate wing in 1800, the Capitol has been a work-in-progress since then. Starting with the laying of the cornerstone by George Washington in 1793, with great pomp through the expansion of the East Front in 1959, changes to the Capitol have been constant. By 1865, the small wooden dome was replaced by the iron dome that makes the Capitol the centerpiece of Washington, D.C., it is today. Today, the entire Capitol complex occupies 3.5 acres; it is 750 feet long and nearly half as wide.

INSIDE THE CAPITOL DOME. When you enter the Capitol Rotunda, your first awe-inspiring experience is located 180 feet above. At the canopy of the Capitol Dome is *The Apotheosis of George Washington*, an allegorical painting featuring George Washington seated in majesty with the Goddess of Liberty on his right and Victory and Fame on his left. The 13 maidens surrounding Washington represent the original states, and they are holding a banner containing the motto "E Pluribus Unum." This phrase, meaning one out of many, refers to the creation of one country from many individual states. The entire fresco is 62 feet and 2 inches in diameter; the figures are 15 feet high and all were painted by Constantino Brumidi between 1863 and 1865.

SITE A5: ATOP THE CAPITOL DOME. The *Statue of Freedom* (designed by Thomas U. Walter in the 1850s) is, at 19.5 feet high, the tallest statue in Washington, D.C. Its sculptor was Thomas Crawford, but then Secretary of War Jefferson Davis suggested a helmet encircled by stars instead of a Liberty Cap as an expression "of endless existence and heavenly birth." Freedom stands on a globe 7 feet in diameter to symbolize vigilance over the world. The statue was erected on December 2, 1863, in a very public ceremony intended to inspire the Union troops. In 1993, it was removed, cleaned, repaired, and reset atop the dome with great care.

SITE A6: THE RICHARD B. RUSSELL SENATE OFFICE BUILDING. This is the first Senate building on your left on Constitution Avenue between Delaware Avenue and First Street NE. Originally called the Old Senate Office Building, it was built in 1908 and occupied by Senate staff on March 5, 1909. Consider walking to the second floor and viewing its rotunda and columns. The name was changed in 1972 to honor the Democratic senator from Georgia known to his colleagues as a "senator's senator." This was the site of many important events: the Army-McCarthy hearings that investigated communists in government in 1954; the Watergate hearings of 1973-74 that led to the resignation of Richard M. Nixon as President on August 9, 1974; the 1987 Iran-Contra hearings in determining that the illegal sales of arms to the Nicaraguan government were being coordinated by Oliver North from the White House; and, most recently, the site of the Clarence Thomas Supreme Court confirmation hearings in 1991 that featured sexual harassment charges from law professor Anita Hill. Also on this site, at C Street and Delaware Avenue NE, stood Fire Engine Company No. 3.

THE EASTERN DISPENSARY. This was the Casualty Hospital's clinic when it was originally located at 217 Delaware Avenue NE.

SITE A7: THE EVERETT M. DIRKSEN SENATE OFFICE BUILDING. The second Senate building along Constitution Avenue, it was erected in 1956 and renamed in 1972 to honor the Republican senator from Illinois who served in the House of Representatives from 1932 to 1949. Dirksen was the Republican minority leader in the Senate from 1959 until his death in 1969 and was particularly known for his oratory and for being an effective legislative tactician. Between the third- and fourth-floor windows are relief panels depicting scenes from American industry representing Shipping, Farming, Manufacturing, Mining, and Lumbering. The bronze and aluminum doors at Constitution Avenue depict the Seal of the United States (center), Equality (left), and Liberty (right).

SITE A8: THE PHILIP HART SENATE OFFICE BUILDING. This third and most recent Senate building was built over a six-year period beginning in 1976. Named for the Democratic senator from Michigan to recognize his reputation as the conscience of the Senate, it is the largest of the Senate buildings and reserved for the more senior senators. Inside in the expansive atrium hangs the massive mobile sculpture, *Mountains and Clouds*, by renowned artist Alexander Calder (another mobile of his appears in the atrium of the National Gallery of Art). This, the artist's last piece, is the only Calder sculpture to feature a stationery object. He died in 1976.

17

SITE A9: THE SEWALL-BELMONT HOUSE AT 144 CONSTITUTION AVENUE NE. Incorporating an earlier structure dating to the late 1600s or early 1700s, Robert Sewall built this Federal period-style house in 1800, thereby making this one of the oldest homes in Washington, D.C. Albert Gallatin, secretary of the treasury under Thomas Jefferson and James Madison, lived here from 1802 through 1813, and it is here where the Louisiana Purchase was drafted. On August 14, 1814, a British invasion force burned the Capitol nearby and set fire to the house. It was the only private home to suffer damage by fire during the invasion. The house was bought in 1929 from Senator Porter Dale as the headquarters of the National Women's Party. Alice Paul, leader of the early suffragette movement and author of the Equal Rights Amendment, occupied the second-floor apartment until her death in 1977 at 92 years old. The house, declared a National Historic Site in 1974, now serves as a museum of artifacts and memorabilia documenting the history of the women's movement. *Open Tuesday through Friday, 10 a.m. to 3 p.m.; Saturday, noon to 4 p.m. Call (202)546-3989 for more information.*

SITE A10: MOUNTJOY BAYLY HOUSE AT 122 MARYLAND NE. Mountjoy Bayly was a doorkeeper and sergeant-at-arms of the early U.S. Senate. In 1929, this Federal-style house was bought by Senator Hiram Johnson of California. A progressive senator from 1917 until 1945, Senator Johnson had been Theodore Roosevelt's vice presidential running mate on the Progressive or "Bull Moose" party ticket of 1912. After Johnson's death, the house was bought in 1947 as headquarters for the General Commission on Chaplain and Armed Forces Personnel. It is now the Washington, D.C. office of the American Civil Liberties Union and is listed in the National Register of Historic Places. *Not open to the public.*

SITE A11: UNITED STATES SUPREME COURT. The Supreme Court had a wandering life for the first 135 years in Washington, D.C. It had met in private homes, taverns, hotels, and several locations within the Capitol itself, usually near the Senate. Only in 1935 was the Court finally provided a permanent location. The plaza in front is 100 feet wide. On the left of the main staircase is *The Contemplation of Justice*, who is holding a statue representing Justice. On the right is *The Authority of Law.* Both were sculpted in marble by James Earle Fraser in 1935. On this site once stood the Old Brick Capitol (shown here). It was built in 1815 as the temporary home of Congress after the British occupied and burned the Capitol on August 24, 1814. A stock company was created to build a temporary meeting site for Congress until the old Capitol could be rebuilt. The Old Brick Capital served Congress until 1819. Pres. James Monroe was inaugurated outside the building on March 4, 1817, marking the first time the oath of office was taken outside. Except on rare occasions, the custom has been maintained ever since.

THE OLD CAPITOL PRISON. Once located here, the prison housed political prisoners during the Civil War, including notorious Confederate spy Rose O'Neal Greenhow. After Congress returned to the refurbished Capitol in December 1819, this building became a private school and a boardinghouse for congressmen. In 1861, the federal government installed wooden bars on the windows and used it as a prison for renegade Union officers, spies, contraband slaves, and political prisoners. The most famous prisoners, both celebrated Confederate spies, were Rose O'Neal Greenhow and Belle Boyd.

SITE A12: THE FOLGER SHAKESPEARE LIBRARY. This is a living museum dedicated to the work and legacy of William Shakespeare. The Elizabethan Theatre is the heart of its living performances with its three-tiered gallery and walls of timber and plaster, all reminiscent of a theatre in the time of Shakespeare. The Folger Reading Room is available by appointment for scholars, graduate students, and the public. The art deco classic building, opened in 1932, was a gift from Henry Clay Folger. His extensive collection of Shakespearean works formed the nucleus of its now massive collection of rare work. *Open 10 a.m. to 4 p.m. Monday through Saturday. Closed on federal holidays. No admission to view the changing exhibit in the front hall. Tours require no prior arrangement and begin Monday through Saturday at 11 a.m.; Tuesdays at 10 a.m. and 11 a.m. The Gardens are open every third Saturday from April through October at 10 a.m. and 11 a.m. Call (202)675-0365 for more tour information.*

GRANT'S ROW. On this site stood 14 of the most expensive brick rowhouses built in Washington east of the Capitol at the time. They were erected in 1871 by Capt. Albert Grant, a Union veteran, who speculated that this area of the city would be the first to develop into a highly desired residential area in Washington. The asking prices were too high and sales never matched expectations. Within a decade, the area became a low- and middle-income neighborhood and rapidly declined. Grant declared bankruptcy, and the rowhouses were bought by Standard Oil president Henry C. Folger in 1928. After the row houses were razed, they were replaced by the Folger Shakespeare Library.

SITE A13: FREDERICK DOUGLASS HOUSE AT 316 A STREET NE. From 1871 through 1878, this was the first Washington home of the famed African-American abolitionist, orator, and diplomat. Later, Douglass and his wife moved to Cedar Hill and a house across the Anacostia River (now a museum run by the National Park Service). Douglass served as the Recorder of Deeds for the District of Columbia and Consul General to Haiti. While living here, Douglass helped dedicate Lincoln Park, about eight blocks farther down East Capitol Street. See detour at Site 17.

SITE A14: FREDERICK DOUGLASS MUSEUM AT 316-318 A STREET NE. From 1964 until 1987, these townhouses served as the Museum of African Art. It was the first museum dedicated to preserving and promoting the study of Sub-Saharan African art, history, and culture. The entire collection was moved to its permanent location near the Smithsonian Castle and on the Mall at 950 Independence Avenue. *Open by appointment only.*

SITE A15: BRUMIDI HOUSE AT 326 A STREET NE. At this wood and stucco home lived the Italian painter Constantino Brumidi, who spent nearly 25 years painting the interior ceilings and walls of the U.S. Capitol until his death in 1880. His work on the rotunda frescos and the friezes are lifelike events depicting the history of the United States; his *Apotheosis of Washington* on the ceiling of the Capitol dome was done in 11 months. Brumidi was once left dangling 60 feet above the brick floor of the Rotunda when his painting chair slipped off the scaffolding. At age 72, this proved to be too much of a strain, and he died a few months later. He is buried in Glenwood Cemetery in Northeast Washington.

SITE A16: ST. MARK'S EPISCOPAL CHURCH AT 3RD AND A STREETS SE. Built in the Romanesque style of architecture in 1888, this church is a well-known Capitol Hill landmark. Many of its worshippers, like Pres. Lyndon B. Johnson, were important movers and shakers of the city. Many people enjoy the gardens during the summer. Inside are stained-glass windows designed by Tiffany.

SITE A17: LIBRARY OF CONGRESS JOHN ADAMS BUILDING. This building became an annex to the Main Library, the Thomas Jefferson Building (in front), when it was built in 1939. Today, this utilitarian government building houses library administrative staff and storage facilities.

CALDWELL HOUSE. When it was razed in 1933 for the John Adams building of the Library of Congress, the Caldwell House was the oldest private home on Capitol Hill. It was built in 1809 by Elios Boudinot Caldwell, chief clerk of the Supreme Court from 1800 until his death in 1825. It was thought to have been the home of the Supreme Court from 1815 through 1817 while the Capitol was being rebuilt after it had been burned by the British invasion in 1814. A receipt was found, however, that recorded the actual site as being at the corner of Independence and New Jersey, the Daniel Carroll house. Still, it is important to note that the Marquis de Lafayette, a longtime friend of Caldwell, spent several days at Caldwell House during his triumphant visit to the United States in 1824.

SITE A18: LIBRARY OF CONGRESS THOMAS JEFFERSON BUILDING. The first library for the exclusive use of Congress was housed in one room of the Capitol and cost $5,000 for its entire collection. Virtually all of the books were lost when the British burned the Capitol in August 1814 in retaliation to the burning of a Canadian library during the War of 1812. After the fire, Thomas Jefferson sold his entire collection to Congress to form the nucleus of the new Library of Congress; unfortunately, most of his collection was subsequently lost in an 1851 fire. After the Capitol was rebuilt, the Library was returned to the Capitol until this permanent building was completed in 1897. Tour the Main Reading Room and the magnificent Great Hall. Atop the building is *The Torch of Learning.* The 23-carat gold leaf overlayed over the copper torch provides a vivid contrast on a clear sunny day. Created by sculptor Edward Pearce Casey in 1893, the torch is 15 feet tall on a base 6.5 feet wide and stands 195 feet high. *Call (202)707-5000 for tour information.*

CARROLL ROW. Five Federal-style townhouses were located on this site. Throughout their existence—from 1805 when they were built until they were razed in 1886 to build the Library of Congress—these townhouses were very much part of the history of Washington, D.C. They were constructed by Daniel Carroll of Duddington, one of the original patent holders whose property included all of Capitol Hill and beyond. The first inaugural ball was held here to honor the inauguration of James Madison in 1809. In 1814, the British invasion force commandeered Dr. Charles Ewing's townhouse for its use to treat British soldiers injured during the attack on Washington that August. Young Abraham Lincoln lived in Mrs. Spratt's boardinghouse while a member of Congress from Illinois from 1847 to 1849. During the Civil War, the townhouses served as Carroll Prison for political prisoners.

SITE A19: THE COURT OF NEPTUNE FOUNTAIN. This wonderfully animated bronze sculpture by Roland Hinton Perry was built in 1897-98 and features a 12-foot King Neptune sitting on the center rock overseeing his underwater kingdom. His sons, the tritons, are calling the sea-people through conch shells to visit with their father. Frogs and turtles spout water while nymphs on seahorses frolic nearby. Neptune, a Roman divinity, was the son of Saturn and Rhea and the brother of Jupiter and Pluto. Each brother chose command over one area of the world by lot, so that Jupiter became king of the heavens, Pluto became king of the underworld, and Neptune became king of the oceans.

SITE A20: LIBRARY OF CONGRESS JAMES MADISON BUILDING. Built in 1980, this is the most recent annex to the Main Library. An entire series of rowhouses dating from about the Civil War was demolished to construct the third annex to the Library of Congress. Today, it houses the great collection of maps, photographs, prints, and films. The exhibit off the main entrance is constantly changing and worth a visit anytime.

SITE A21: JOSEPH CANNON HOUSE OFFICE BUILDING. This is the first of three office buildings that house the offices for the members of the House of Representatives, as well as various committee rooms and staff offices. It was an attempt to relieve overcrowding in the Capitol and keep members from having to rent office space or work from home. "Uncle Joe" Cannon, the autocratic Speaker of the House from 1903 until 1911, laid the cornerstone for the House Office Building on April 15, 1906. Today, "junior" members of the House are given offices here. Uncle Joe, serving his Illinois district for 46 years from 1873 until 1923 (he was out of office for two terms), died in 1926. The Joseph Holt House, named for the judge who sentenced Mary Surratt to hang for her part in the assassination of Abraham Lincoln, was located here from 1795 until 1904.

HENRY BROCK'S CONGRESSIONAL HOTEL. Most of Capitol Hill in this area was taken up by hotels, boardinghouses, and taverns. On this site stood a Victorian-style, three-story brick building known as the Congressional Hotel. While a 1903 photograph exists, it is not known when the structure was built. It was probably razed along with similar buildings for the Cannon House Office Building.

SITE A22: NICHOLAS LONGWORTH HOUSE OFFICE BUILDING. This is the second building erected for use by members of the House of Representatives. Named to honor Speaker of the House Nicholas Longworth of New York, this building was dedicated in 1929. Longworth was a member of the House from 1903 to 1913 and again from 1915 until his death in 1931. Today, the "sophomore" class of the House are provided offices here, just one step above the older Cannon Building. On this site stood the Carroll-Mills House, a rental home owned by David Carroll of Duddington, one of the original landowners of Jenkins Hill. It was probably built in the late 1790s. The Supreme Court used the house as a temporary court from December 1814 to December 1815 after the British invasion burned their offices in the Capitol. This is known from a receipt signed by Washington Boyd, marshal of the Supreme Court. From 1836 to 1855, it was the home of Robert Mills, the architect who designed the Washington Monument and the Treasury Building, among others. The house was razed in 1873 to build the Butler House.

BUTLER HOUSE. This was the site of the home built for Maj. Gen. Benjamin F. Butler, the Union general in 1873. It was Butler who declared that escaped slaves were "contraband of war" and therefore free; he also believed that any woman who showed any discourtesy to a Union soldier was considered to be a prostitute "plying her trade" and should be treated "accordingly." For these and other statements, he was nicknamed "Beast" Butler when he was military governor of New Orleans in 1862. Preferring to remain in the field with his command, he declined to run with Lincoln as vice president in 1864 and instead Andrew Johnson succeeded to the presidency after Lincoln's assassination in 1865. After the war, Butler was elected as a Republican to Congress where he led the impeachment against Pres. Andrew Johnson. He served briefly as governor of Massachusetts, then returned to Washington to live in his Italianate mansion. He died in 1893. The house was sold and used as government office space until it was razed for the Longworth House Office Building in 1928.

SITE A23: SAM RAYBURN HOUSE

OFFICE BUILDING. The third and most recent House office building was named for Speaker of the House Sam Rayburn of Texas. Rayburn served in the House from 1913 until his death in 1961 and was its Speaker from 1940 until 1961. The mixture of modern and Neo-classical building design proved very costly and received considerable criticism. The large marble sculptures on the main entrance facing Independence Avenue represent, on the left, *The Spirit of Justice*, and, on the right, *The Majesty of Law*. On the west and east facade are 9-feet-high Greek vases modeled after the Greek drinking horn. Other adornments throughout the building, such as the Great Seal of the United States and a lion panel, add to the Neo-classical design. This building is reserved for the "senior" members of the House of Representatives because of its close proximity to the Capitol.

SITE A24: BARTHOLDI FOUNTAIN.

This cast-iron fountain coated with bronze was the pride and wonder of the Philadelphia Centennial Exhibition of 1876. The federal government bought the entire fountain for $6,000 and erected it on the grounds of the Botanic Garden when the garden was located in the center of the Mall. In the early 1930s, the Botanic Garden relocated across the street, and, in 1932, the fountain followed. The sculptor was Frederic Auguste Bartholdi, famous for his 1886 design of the *Statue of Liberty* in New York Harbor. The fountain is 30 feet high and weighs 15,000 pounds (7.5 tons). The wide marble basin itself is 90 feet wide. Three 11-foot-high "caryatids" support the 13-foot-wide basin at the top from which 12 Victorian electric lamps are suspended. These electric lamps caused quite a stir in the late 19th century, since it was the earliest public display of electric lights in the city. Above the basin are three young tritons kneeling to support the upper fountain. The small building just behind the fountain originally served as the office of the garden director when it was built in 1932. Today, it houses administrative staff for the Botanic Garden.

ings were seventy feet high top of the balustrade, and ntral dome, which was con-ed of wood with a covering pper, was seventy-five feet

ntil 1851 nothing of conse- e was done to the exterior
NATIONAL BOTANICAL GARI
e Capitol, but its architect, rt Mills, made some slight improvements to the interior. ed to build greater wings or extensions north and south houses might be better accommodated, and accordingly, c ly, 1851, the corner-stone of the south extension was nic rites. President Fillmore participated in the ceren tary of State Daniel Webster delivered an oration. A d as follows, was placed under the corner-stone:

On the morning of the first day of the seventy-sixth y pendence of the United States of America, in the city of W

SITE A25: BOTANIC GARDEN. George Washington recommended that a botanic garden be built and maintained by the federal government. In 1842, the Wilkes Exploring Expedition returned with rare plants from Fiji, New Zealand, and South America. They were transplanted successfully to the Botanic Garden in 1850 when the Botanic Garden was located in the center of the Mall. The entire building was moved to its present location in 1934. These new plant species formed the basis of the first serious collection of tropical plants that now number in the hundreds. The best part is that visitors can enjoy these tropical delights every day of the year. Also, experimentation and botanic research are a part of the garden's mission. The variety of horticultural displays should not be missed. *Open to the public every day from 9 a.m. to 5 p.m.*

SITE A26: PRESIDENT JAMES ABRAM GARFIELD MEMORIAL. After only three months in office, President Garfield, the 20th president, was shot and killed by a disappointed office-seeker at the Baltimore and Potomac Railroad Station on September 19, 1881. The train station, less than a mile west of this memorial, is now the site of the National Gallery of Art. Garfield was a Republican member of the U.S. House of Representatives from Ohio, serving from 1863 until his election to the presidency in 1881. During the Civil War, Garfield commanded an infantry regiment and was appointed chief of staff of the Army of the Cumberland until he resigned to run for Congress. The 9-foot-tall bronze statue of Garfield, sculpted by John Quincy Adams Ward, was erected by his old comrades of the Army of the Cumberland. He faces west and holds his inaugural address in his left hand. The marble pedestal features three allegorical Roman figures representing Garfield's three careers as soldier, scholar, and statesman.

SITE A27A: GENERAL ULYSSES S. GRANT MEMORIAL. Of all the statues in Washington, D.C., this grouping by sculptor Henry Merwin Shrady is the largest, most expensive, and assuredly one of the most important. Dedicated on April 27, 1922, the centennial of Grant's birth, the sculpture is in three distinct parts. The central equestrian statue is 17.2 feet high, weighs 10,700 pounds, and rests on a marble pedestal that is 22.5 feet tall. Grant is depicted sitting calmly with slouched shoulders, observing a battle in progress somewhere in the distance. The central Grant memorial was completed in 1920. Taken together, the monument measures 252 feet long and 71 feet wide. On the day the memorial was to be dedicated, Vice Pres. Calvin Coolidge (Pres. Warren G. Harding was dedicating Grant's birthplace at Point Pleasant, Ohio, that day) and General of the Armies John J. Pershing both gave dedication addresses. It was an elaborate ceremony, complete with a military parade from the White House to the Capitol. Sculptor Henry Shrady unfortunately was unable to attend the dedication of the massive monument that he worked for 20 years to complete. He had died two weeks earlier from overwork.

GENERAL ULYSSES S. GRANT. Grant, shown here in uniform as commander-in-chief of the Union Forces in 1864, was a West Point graduate who served during the Mexican War until 1854, when he re-entered civilian life. At the outbreak of the Civil War in 1861, Grant re-enlisted as colonel of the Illinois volunteer regiment and became brevet brigadier general of all volunteers in August 1861. As a brevet major general in 1862, Grant was in command at Shiloh and captured Vicksburg in 1863. Promoted to regular army lieutenant general in March 1864 with command of all Union forces, Grant accepted Gen. Robert E. Lee's surrender of all Confederate forces at Appomattox Court House on April 9, 1865, which effectively ended the Civil War. Grant became interim secretary of war in 1867. In 1868, he was elected the 18th president of the United States and was re-elected in 1872. Upon retiring from the presidency, Grant eventually settled in New York City and, after the collapse of his investment business, wrote his memoirs; they were completed only four days before he died in 1885. Grant is buried in New York City.

SITE A27B: GRANT MEMORIAL: THE ARTILLERY GROUP. To the right, or south, is the *Artillery Group*, comprised of a caisson, carrying a cannon and three soldiers and being pulled by three horses. The expressions on each of the men each show the strain of battle in different ways. Actual West Point cadets were used as models for these soldiers, and their names appear on a plaque at the rear of this statue group: Fairfax Ayres, James E. Chaney, and Henry Weeks. The horses themselves, like the ones carved for the Cavalry Group, are carved in such exquisite detail as to appear almost alive. The *Artillery Group* was finally lowered into place in 1912.

SITE A27C: GRANT MEMORIAL: THE CAVALRY GROUP. To the left, or north, is the *Cavalry Group*, comprised of seven soldiers of a cavalry regiment charging onto a field of battle. When the commission was granted in 1902 to a self-taught and relatively unknown sculptor, it caused a furor by more established artists and sculptors. He watched numerous military parades and devoted an enormous amount of time to studying Civil War history, military uniforms, and military practices. The *Cavalry Group* was lowered into place in 1916.

SITE A28: THE OLMSTEAD FOUNTAIN. This fountain was connected to the underground springs that refreshed Capitol Hill since the late 18th century. A version of the spring can be seen in the grotto nearby. Although the history of the fountain is not clear, it was probably named for Frederick Law Olmstead, the internationally renowned landscape architect known for creating, among others, the grounds of the Capitol and Central Park in New York City. Olmstead died in 1903.

SITE A29: PEACE MONUMENT. Dedicated in 1877, this 40-foot-high memorial honors the loss of the Union naval defenders during the Civil War. It was created from a rough sketch done by Adm. David Porter and executed by sculptor Franklin Simmons. At the top of the memorial, America weeps on the shoulders of History while recording the heroes in her book. The inscription is "They died that their country might live." In the center of the marble pedestal, Victory holds a laurel wreath and an oak branch over the infant Neptune (god of the sea) and Mars (god of war) to crown the sacrifices of all sailors who were involved in naval maneuvers during the Civil War. On the back of the statue, Peace extends an olive branch. Science, Literature, and Art symbolize the progress that comes with Peace.

SITE A30: CAPITOL GROTTO. The entire grounds of the U.S. Capitol were designed by the internationally renowned landscape architect Frederick Law Olmstead, also known for designing New York City's Central Park in the mid-1870s. During this period, the Capitol grounds hosted croquet games and Easter egg rolls, and, according to an 1877 report, stray cows who damaged the plants and bushes. The brick enclosure to this grotto was created in 1879 as a refreshment site for fresh water. This spring was apparently used by Indians when they camped at the foot of Jenkins Hill and also by travelers headed to Georgetown and points west. This is the grotto made famous as one of the midnight meeting places between Bob Woodward and Carl Bernstein of the *Washington Post* and their Watergate source known only as "Deep Throat." The ensuing investigation of White House wiretapping and the break-in at the Watergate office building in 1973 led to the resignation of Pres. Richard M. Nixon on August 9, 1974, marking the first time an American president has resigned.

SITE A31: ROBERT A. TAFT MEMORIAL. Considered by his peers to be "Mr. Republican," the Ohio senator was first elected to the Senate in 1932 where he served until his death in 1953. Taft was an adamant opponent of Pres. Franklin D. Roosevelt and his New Deal programs. The 11-foot bronze statue is overshadowed by the 100-foot-high, 27-bell carillon that chimes every 15 minutes.

FIRST BALTIMORE AND OHIO DEPOT IN WASHINGTON, D.C. 1835
PENNA. AVENUE AND SECOND ST. NW — N.W. CORNER

SITE A32A: BALTIMORE AND OHIO RAILROAD DEPOT. This drawing was made of the first depot of the B&O railroad station located here from 1835 until 1852. It was one of two separate railroad lines serving Washington, D.C., throughout the 19th century. The other was the Baltimore and Potomac railroad station located at Constitution and Sixth Streets, now the site of the National Gallery of Art. (See Site C9.)

ARRIVAL OF THE NEW YORK SEVENTY-FIRST REGIMENT AT THE RAILROAD DEPOT, WASHINGTON, D. C.—FROM A SKETCH BY OUR SPECIAL ARTIST.

ANOTHER BALTIMORE AND OHIO RAILROAD DEPOT. This newer B&O railroad station was built on the same site in 1852 and served until the completion of Union Station in 1907. Built in an Italianate style, the clock tower became a local landmark. It was here that President Lincoln arrived in disguise in the early morning for his inauguration in 1861 and, sadly, it was from here that his funeral train departed for Illinois in April 1865.

AN 1887 TRAIN ACCIDENT. One of the great hazards involving a train station located along a busy city street is the constant threat of accidents involving trains, carriages, and people. This train accident on August 17, 1887, in Washington, D.C., involving a B&O train demonstrates this hazard rather effectively. Apparently, there were more than 30 accidents each year involving pedestrians who were killed or hurt along the train route. The smoke, noise, coal piles, lumber yards, and other railroad facilities located in and around the Mall and residential areas were a constant irritant to those who had to work and live nearby. The 1901 McMillan Plan helped usher in the new Union Station in 1907 and helped to consolidate the two competing stations and finally eliminated the clutter and noise of the railroad stations. Still, it must have been quite a sight to see a full train coming down through city streets.

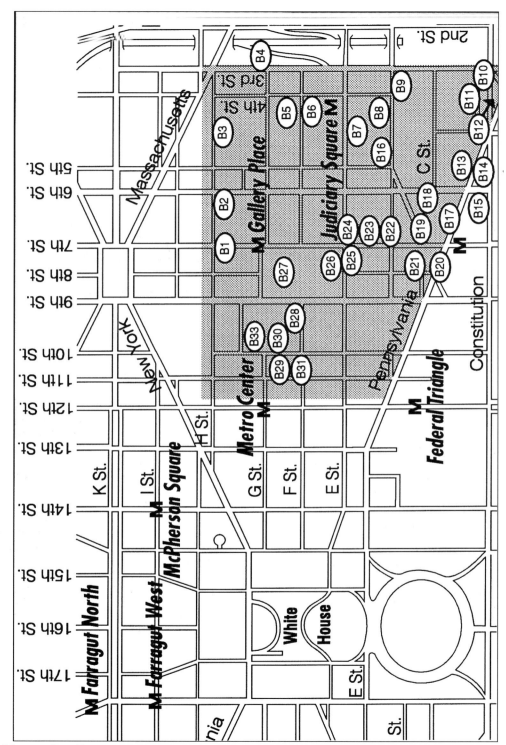

MAP OF OLD DOWNTOWN.

Tour B

OLD DOWNTOWN

"The grand avenu[e] connecting both the palace and the Federal House . . . will offer a variety of situation unparalleled in point of beauties . . ."
—Pierre L'Enfant describing Pennsylvania Avenue, 1791

Pennsylvania Avenue was intended to be the grand avenue that would serve as a symbolic connection between the White House and the Congress. North of "The Avenue," as the early locals called it, was the residential section; the Mall was to the south. "People of distinction" lived north of the Avenue.

Before the Civil War, the area east of the White House and north of the Mall was its own distinctive neighborhood, consisting of small shops and homes of important politicians, statesmen, and the ordinary family. But by the advent of streetcars and train stations in the 1880s, the area slowly became the commercial heart of the city for the next 50 years.

From 1880 until 1920, this area we are calling Old Downtown consisted roughly of Pennsylvania Avenue (the original Main Street of Washington), F Street (it is on higher ground and easier to pass year-round between Georgetown and the Capitol), and 7th Street (which was intended as the main commercial street north of the Mall).

Today and ever since the Federal Triangle project began construction in 1935, government buildings have become the norm in Old Downtown, especially around Pennsylvania Avenue. Judiciary Square still maintains its early history as the seat of justice for Washington, D.C., while the convention center, museums, and busy freeways now intersect the area. The community, however, still retains some of its early history of small shops and historic homes.

SITE B1: THE CHINATOWN FRIENDSHIP ARCH ON H STREET BETWEEN SEVENTH AND EIGHTH STREETS. Two of the world's leading capitals are symbolically joined in friendship through this wonderfully colored, Baroque arch. Beijing, the capital of China, presented this arch designed by Alfred Liu in 1986 and incorporating Chinese art from the Ming and Ch'ing Dynasties to the United States. It is considered to be one of the largest Chinese arches outside China. Chinatown today generally encompasses a neighborhood stretching between H and K Streets NW and between Sixth and Ninth Streets NW. You can tell when you're there because the street signs are in both English and Chinese characters. Until 1935, however, Chinatown was located at C Street and Pennsylvania Avenue, around the current sites of the Federal Courthouse and the Embassy of Canada. The Chinatown community moved to this new area when the federal buildings started appearing around them.

SITE B2: MARY SURRATT BOARDING HOUSE AT 604 H STREET. Here is the boardinghouse of Mary Surratt, who was hanged as a co-conspirator for the assassination of Abraham Lincoln on April 14, 1865, at Ford's Theater. The seven Lincoln conspirators—John Wilkes Booth, George Atzerodt, Lewis Payne, David Herald, Edward Spangler, Michael O'Laughlin, and Samuel B. Arnold—met here for several months to plan the assassinations of Lincoln, Vice Pres. Andrew Johnson, and Secretary of State William Seward. The assassination of Lincoln succeeded, of course, but Seward escaped with only injuries from a botched knife attack. Johnson was unharmed. The conspirators were easily caught and hanged at Fort McNair on July 9, 1865.

SITE B3: THE GENERAL ACCOUNTING OFFICE AT FOURTH AND H STREETS. Created in 1921, the "GAO," as it is sometimes affectionately called, is charged with " . . . auditing the accounts of the Federal Government, and with adjusting and settling . . . all claims and demands made by or against the United States Government." The George McLellan House at 334 H Street also stood here. On this site, McClellan was given command of the Army of the Potomac by Pres. Abraham Lincoln and his chief of staff, Henry Halleck, on September 2, 1862. McClellan was charged with the protection of the capital, but his army rarely saw battle. He was later dismissed by Lincoln for his inability to take command more aggressively.

SITE B4: LILLIAN AND ALBERT SMALL JEWISH MUSEUM AND JEWISH HISTORICAL CENTER AT 701 THIRD STREET. This is considered to be the oldest existing synagogue in Washington, D.C. Built between 1873 and 1876, the groundbreaking of the building was attended by President Grant. Al Jolson, the star of the first "talkie" picture, *The Jazz Singer*, sang in the choir here while his father served as the rabbi to the relocated Adas Israel Synagogue. Today, the building is a National Historic Shrine, providing research into the Jewish life of Washington, D.C., and throughout the United States.

SITE B5: THE NATIONAL BUILDING MUSEUM AT 441 G STREET. For nearly 60 years, this huge building processed pensions for veterans from the Revolutionary War to WW I. Later, the General Accounting Office and the post office both occupied the Old Pension Building at one time or another after WW II. Designed by U.S. Army General M.C. Meigs, an engineer and architect, the building was dedicated in 1883 as a memorial to the veterans of the Civil War. The terra-cotta sculptures surrounding the frieze depict a number of military units such as medical, quartermaster, artillery, infantry, and others. Its huge interior has hosted numerous presidential inaugural balls since 1885. Since 1980, the National Building Museum, dedicated to the architectural history of the United States, has been located here. *Open to the public. Call (202) 272-2448.* Also on this site stood the City Jail. At the corner of Fourth and G Streets NW on the site of the National Building Museum was the original jail of the District of Columbia designed by George Hadfield in 1801. By 1839, overcrowding required the building of a new jail nearby. The original jail was used as the Washington Infirmary but was destroyed by fire in 1861. The second jail was torn down in 1874.

SITE B6: THE NATIONAL LAW ENFORCEMENT OFFICERS MEMORIAL ON F STREET BETWEEN FOURTH AND FIFTH STREETS AT JUDICIARY SQUARE METRO STATION. Similar in concept to the Vietnam War Memorial, this newest memorial is carved with the names of 12,561 police officers killed in the line of duty. It was dedicated to these officers by Pres. George Bush on October 15, 1991. Christian Hines remembers on the square "bounded by E and F and Fourth and Fifth streets, an old tobacco house" was located between 1790 and 1800. Also, "on Judiciary Square, an old tobacco or farm-house [was] occupied by Mr. Brown."

SITE B7: THE DISTRICT OF COLUMBIA COURTHOUSE ON D STREET BETWEEN FOURTH AND FIFTH STREETS. When the central section of this Greek Revival building was erected from a design by George Hadfield in 1820, it served as Washington's first city hall. The east wing (facing the Capitol) was added in 1826; the west wing was added in 1846. Until 1850, an occasional slave auction was held at the site. During the Civil War, it was used as a Union hospital and government offices. Since 1863, this has been the seat of the District Court with jurisdiction for federal cases as well. It was here that Charles Guiteau was tried for the assassination of President Garfield in 1881. Christian Hines remembers on the square "bounded by D and E and Third and Fourth streets, a three-story brick house occupied by a Mr. Young."

SITE B8: ABRAHAM LINCOLN STATUE ON D STREET BETWEEN FOURTH AND FIFTH STREETS. Within three years after Lincoln's assassination, this marble statue by sculptor Lot Flannery was erected as the first memorial to the martyred president. Originally, the statue stood on a column some 40 feet high. We do know that the statue was removed when the courthouse was enlarged in 1920, and the memorial was not expected to be returned to the site because a larger memorial was under construction on the East Mall. Still, the public outcry was so great that the statue was returned, although on a lower, simpler pedestal, in 1923.

Site B9: Brigadier General Albert Pike Statue on Third and D Streets.

An independent and intellectual man for his times, Albert Pike was a powerful newspaper editor whose opinions carried great political weight, especially while he was advocating a transcontinental railroad. He was a veteran of the Mexican and Civil Wars; in the latter, he served as a Confederate general who lost his only engagement. While this is the only memorial honoring a Confederate general in Washington, sculptor Gaetano Trentanove portrays Pike not as a Confederate but as a leader of the Scottish Rite Masonic organization where Pike was considered to be one of the chief interpreters of the highly secretive Masonic rite during his life. At the base of the 11-foot bronze statue is the goddess of masonry holding the banner of the Scottish Rite. Dedicated in 1901, it was temporarily moved during the construction of Metrorail in 1975 before being returned to its original setting.

Site B10: Sir William Blackstone Statue at Constitution Avenue and Third Street.

His very name evokes the standard of law practiced for the past 250 years. *Blackstone's Commentaries* is a compilation of clarified English laws and of Blackstone's lectures as Oxford's first full professor of law beginning in 1758. This 9-foot bronze statue of William Blackstone celebrates our system of law that began with the legal traditions of Great Britain. It was presented by the wife of sculptor Paul Wayland Bartlett at its dedication in 1943.

SITE B11: TRYLON OF FREEDOM ON CONSTITUTION AVENUE BETWEEN THIRD AND FOURTH STREETS. Just in front of the E. Barrett Prettyman Federal Court Building, a three-sided, 24-foot granite sculpture by Carl Paul Jennewein features bas relief representations of the freedoms exemplified by the Constitution and the Declaration of Independence. The three sides symbolically represent the three branches of government: legislative, judicial, and executive. The southwest side, for example, shows the freedoms of press, speech, and religion. The southeast side shows the trial by jury, the lawyer counseling his defendant, and a wharf depicting the elimination of illegal search and seizure. The north side shows the Great Seal of the U.S. superimposed on the Declaration of Independence and the Constitution. The Trylon and courthouse dedication is shown here in 1954.

SITE B12: THE GEORGE GORDON MEADE STATUE. Charles A. Grafy designed this marble memorial to the Civil War Union general in 1927. It originally stood on the site of the National Gallery of Art East Building. The memorial was moved here c. 1984. During the move, the gilded wreath was lost and this reproduction was made. General Meade, commander of the Army of the Potomac and hero of Gettysburg, died in 1872.

SITE B13: EMBASSY OF CANADA AT 501 PENNSYLVANIA AVENUE NW. Pierre L'Enfant would have been very pleased with the placement of this embassy along Pennsylvania Avenue. He envisioned Pennsylvania Avenue and the West Mall area as "Embassy Row" in his early plans for the Federal City. So far this is the only embassy along "The Avenue." It caused something of a stir when it was dedicated in 1989 not only for its placement, but also for its fresh, open style. Designed by Arthur Erikson, the 12 columns in the inner courtyard represent Canada's ten provinces and two territories. All of this is quite a change over the parking lot shown in this 1942 photo. The lot has since been replaced by John Marshall Park and the embassy site. *Open for self-guided tours for rotating art exhibits Mon-Fri from 10 a.m. to 5 p.m. Other business requires an appointment.*

THE NATIONAL HOTEL, 1826–1942. On this site stood six connected, Federal-style townhouses standing five stories tall. They were originally called Weightman's Row, named after Roger C. Weightman, whose residence and bookstore were originally located here beginning in 1818. In 1826, John Gadsby, of Gadsby's Tavern in Alexandria, bought the complex and oversaw the 200-room National Hotel until 1836 when his son John took it over. For nearly 100 years, until it closed in 1921, the National Hotel was one of the most fashionable hotels of its day. Charles Dickens wrote about the hotel in his *American Notes* in 1841. Andrew Jackson, James Buchanan, Henry Clay, Abraham Lincoln, John Wilkes Booth, and many other historical personages frequented the National Hotel to make it one of the most historical sites in Washington, despite the annual floods. After the hotel was closed in 1921, the building was used for district offices until it was finally razed as a fire hazard in 1942.

SITE B14: THE ANDREW W. MELLON MEMORIAL FOUNTAIN AT CONSTITUTION AND PENNSYLVANIA AVENUES. Look directly into the third circular pool of water to see the signs of the Zodiac carved in granite. Sculptor Sidney Waugh designed each of the signs to face the sun in correspondence to the time the stars representing the sign appear overhead. The fountain was dedicated by friends of Andrew Mellon in 1952 to commemorate his extraordinary gifts of both his personal art collection and the building that established the National Gallery of Art across the street in 1937. Mellon's son Paul added to the collection with a sizable bequest of paintings when he died in February 1999.

SITE B15: FEDERAL TRADE COMMISSION (FTC) AT PENNSYLVANIA AND SIXTH STREET. The rounded Doric columns recall the Art Deco period of the 1920s. This federal agency was created by Congress in 1914, and the building was opened in 1938. Notice the four different limestone bas relief sculptures that measure 12 feet wide by 7 feet high. Each depicts a symbol of trade such as *Industry* (two steel workers), *Shipping* (two merchants moving cargo), *Agriculture* (the trade of wheat), and *Foreign Trade* (the now-banned ivory trade in Africa). On the eastern facade are two statues of *Man Controlling Trade*, symbolically represented by the FTC restraining monopolies. Completed in 1942, each are 15 feet long and 12 feet high and carved in limestone.

SITE B16: THE JOSEPH DARLINGTON FOUNTAIN AT FIFTH AND D STREETS IN JUDICIARY PARK. Here the simple, gilded bronze female and the shy fawn symbolize the character of Joseph Darlington (1849–1923), a prominent attorney and respected member of the D.C. Bar Association, to his friends of the Washington Bar Association, who erected this memorial to him in 1923. He led a life of religious conviction with deep professional integrity and personal honesty. He was a tireless teacher and a brilliant lawyer throughout his life. Rest and reflect at the marble pool of water at the base of this simple memorial.

McGIRK'S JAIL. Christian Hines remembers that on the square "between C and D and Fifth and Sixth Streets, a small one-story brick house, in which McGirk was confined, and then known as McGirk's Jail." Not much else is known about Mr. McGirk.

SITE B17: SEARS HOUSE AT 633 PENNSYLVANIA AVENUE. This building is actually three buildings comprised of the twin-towered building of granite and ashlar in front, built in 1888, and the two separate buildings adjoining it to the rear (the Brady Building), built in 1859-60. All three buildings were renovated as one complete building in 1984. Throughout its history, the Central National Bank and the Apex Liquor Store occupied the site as a storefront until Sears and Roebuck Company made this their Washington headquarters. Since 1996, it has been the headquarters of the National Council of Negro Women. On the top three floors of the building next door at 627 Pennsylvania Avenue was the studio of Mathew Brady, the famed Civil War photographer. His glass-plate photography replaced the daguerreotype. This advance allowed more than one image to be made from one negative. Brady went bankrupt in 1880 and worked for other studios until his death in 1896. His collection of Civil War images is still considered the most important work of early photography. Brady is buried in Congressional Cemetery in Washington, D.C.

SITE B17: THE INDIAN QUEEN HOTEL/BROWN'S HOTEL IN 1851. A hotel of one name or another has stood on this site since 1802. The venerable Indian Queen Hotel traces its beginnings to 1810 when manager Jesse Brown enlarged the Davis Hotel on the northwest corner of Pennsylvania Avenue and Sixth Streets NW. In 1820, Brown added a very colorful sign featuring Pocohontas out front and named the hotel Brown's Indian Queen Hotel. The "Star-spangled Banner" was sung at the hotel for the first time in 1814. John Tyler took the oath of office here in 1841 after the unexpected death of William Henry Harrison, and Abraham Lincoln stayed here as a congressman in 1847. In 1851, the hotel was enlarged and renamed Brown's Marble Hotel, but it was sold out of the family in 1865. The new owners changed the name to the Metropolitan Hotel and stayed in business until the building was razed in 1935.

47

SITE B18: THE STEPHENSON GRAND ARMY OF THE REPUBLIC MEMORIAL AT SEVENTH AND C STREETS. This memorial honors Dr. Benjamin F. Stephenson, the founder of the Grand Army of the Republic (GAR), the organization for Civil War veterans. This 25-foot granite memorial features Fraternity (a soldier and sailor), Loyalty (a woman with a drawn sword and a shield), and Charity (a woman protecting a child), all done in bronze. A portrait in bronze of Stephenson appears beneath Fraternity. From 1866 until the early 20th century, the GAR was a potent political force, lobbying for generous pensions, helping widows, and caring for permanently wounded soldiers. The organization was dissolved after the last Union veteran, Albert Woolson, died in 1959 at the age of 109.

SITE B19: TEMPERANCE FOUNTAIN AT SEVENTH AND PENNSYLVANIA AVENUE. San Francisco dentist Henry Cogswell provided this unique bronze-and-granite fountain, *c.* 1880, to help cool people and quench their thirst with water rather than alcohol. Originally, there were water troughs along the base for horses to drink as well. The water crane on top came to symbolize "the purity of water over liquor." Ironically, the memorial stood for many years in front of a liquor store until the old Apex building (the building with turrets) was renovated in the late 1980s to become the Washington headquarters for the Sears Company. Naturally, similar memorials were created for Buffalo, San Francisco, Boston, and others cities.

SITE B20: MAJ. GEN. WINFIELD SCOTT HANCOCK MEMORIAL AT PENNSYLVANIA AVENUE AND SEVENTH STREET. In the 1880 presidential election, General Hancock lost to James A. Garfield by only 10,000 votes. Hancock's distinctive service in the Mexican War and his brilliant Civil War victory at the Battle of Gettysburg helped him achieve national fame and prompted his run for the presidency. The bronze sculpture by Henry Jackson Ellicott captures General Winfield in a commanding pose and seems to accentuate his nickname as "Hancock the Superb." The memorial was dedicated in 1896, ten years after the general's death, in a ceremony attended by Pres. Grover Cleveland.

SITE B21: THE NAVY MEMORIAL ON PENNSYLVANIA AVENUE BETWEEN SEVENTH AND EIGHTH STREETS. This incredible outdoor sculpture features the largest map of the world in stone. The lone sailor created by sculptor Stanley Blyfield represents every sailor since the Revolutionary War. The entire memorial was dedicated in 1987 with an auditorium, gift shop, and hands-on exhibits completely underground. *Open to the public.* On this site also stood three large, 18th-century, Federal-style townhouses owned by the Dermott Family and used as boardinghouses until Avenue House was built as a hotel in 1851. In 1865, all of the small shops on the ground floor were leased to William B. Moses and used as one large furniture store until he moved to larger quarters at F and Eleventh Streets in 1884. Avenue House was demolished in 1885 for the site of the first Saks Clothing Store, which later moved to Fifth Avenue in New York. The building was then occupied by Kann's Department Store. One of the largest department stores in Washington when it opened in 1886, Kann's incorporated four individually distinctive commercial buildings, including the first Woodward & Lothrop Department Store (then known as the Boston Dry Goods Store in 1880) and the first Saks clothing store (now known as Saks Fifth Avenue). The building was finally razed in 1979 after a mysterious fire damaged the entire block.

SITE B22: ALEXANDER GARDNER'S PHOTOGRAPHIC STUDIO ON THE NORTHEAST CORNER OF SEVENTH AND D STREETS. After managing Mathew Brady's photographic studio at Sixth and Pennsylvania at the beginning of the Civil War, Alexander Gardner left the studio to work with the Army of the Potomac. He soon left the service to open his own studio first at 352 Pennsylvania Avenue and then, by 1863, at this site above Shepard & Riley's bookstore. Gardner is best known for photographs that show the wounded and the dead on the battle field: the reality of war. Brady was known for his buildings, sweeping views, and military commanders: the niceties of war. Gardner captured many photographs of Abraham Lincoln, including a famous one taken only four days before the famous assassination. In that photo, a crack appeared in the negative along the president's head that mirrored the path taken by the assassin's bullet. Gardner died in 1882 and is buried in Glenwood Cemetery in Washington, D.C.

SITE B23: ODD FELLOWS HALL AT 423 SEVENTH STREET. The original hall for the Order of Odd Fellows was an elaborate three-story, Second-Empire-style building inspired by the Corcoran Gallery of Art on Lafayette Square. Built in 1845, the original building was razed in 1917 for this new seven-story structure. Odd Fellows, a secret organization similar to the Masons, was founded in England in the 18th century as a benevolent society dedicated to helping its members in sickness and death. Thomas Wildey founded the American chapter in Baltimore after emigrating from England in 1819. The Washington chapter began in 1828.

SITE B24: CLARA BARTON'S BOARDING HOUSE AT 437 SEVENTH STREET. Clara Barton, the founder and first president of the American Red Cross from 1881 to 1904, first lived here while attending the wounded as a relief worker during the Civil War. She then moved to a house at T Street NW where she lived from 1886 until her house was completed near the Cabin John Bridge in 1897. Barton died on Easter Sunday in 1912. The General Services Administration now owns this historic site and is considering plans to restore it into a museum.

SITE B25: THE LANSBURGH BUILDING AT 450 SEVENTH STREET. The Lansburgh department store operated here from 1916 to 1970. The city used the building for arts groups until the Shakespeare Theater moved from the Folger Shakespeare Library site on Capitol Hill to this location in 1987. The building was completely renovated in 1991. The facades remained intact during this project, which also incorporated several adjacent buildings into one commercial and residential structure.

Site B26: The Tariff Commission Building on the Northeast Corner of Eighth and E Streets. Built from 1836 until 1867 according to a design by Robert Mills, this was the original Post Office Building until the existing Old Post Office on Pennsylvania and Twelfth Streets opened in 1899. It is now a commercial building of shops and restaurants. Here, Samuel F.B. Morse operated the first telegraph office in the country.

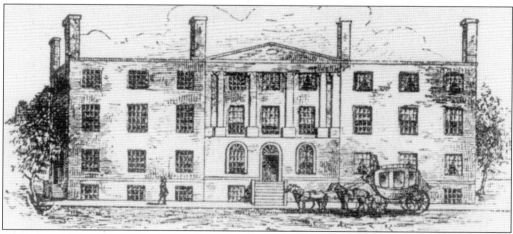

Blodgett's Hotel, 1793–1836. Actually, despite its name, this building was never used as a hotel. It was intended to be the first prize in a lottery scheme advanced by Samuel Blodgett Jr., who made his fortune in the East India trade. He came to Washington in 1792 to help develop this city of several hundred residents. His idea was to hold a lottery that would help raise enough money to develop the public buildings and infrastructure of the new national capital. Although there were lesser prizes of large and small homes, the first prize was Blodgett's Hotel worth $50,000. Overextended and using his land as collateral, Blodgett lost everything and went to debtor's prison. He died in 1814. In 1800, after the failure of the unfinished hotel, the United States Theater moved in and became the first theater company of Washington. The federal government used it as the Post Office Department and Patents Office beginning in 1810. After the British burned the White House and Capitol in 1814, the hotel temporarily became the site for Congress until they moved to the Old Brick Capitol (located on the Supreme Court site). In 1836, the hotel was accidentally set on fire and destroyed. The Tariff Building replaced the old Blodgett's Hotel.

SITE B27: NATIONAL PORTRAIT GALLERY AND NATIONAL MUSEUM OF AMERICAN ART AT EIGHTH AND F STREETS. This is the Old Patent Office building where the early documents of the Republic (the Declaration of Independence, the Constitution, etc. . .) were stored until the National Archives was built in 1934. The building also served as a Civil War hospital and held a number of federal offices until, in 1968, the Smithsonian created the Portrait Gallery and a museum dedicated to American Art. Inside are public bathrooms and a public cafeteria. *Open to the public from 10 a.m. to 5:30 p.m. Closed on Christmas Day. Call (202)357-2700.*

SITE B28: METROPOLITAN THEATRE AT 932 F STREET. The year 1927 featured the very first "talkie" motion picture, *The Jazz Singer*. On this site, the Washington premiere of that historic picture featuring a local boy as its star, Al Jolson, took place. His father was Rabbi of the Talmud Torah Synagogue. The Great Metropolitan Theatre was built in 1918 and featured stage and screen productions up to WW II. Then, in 1928, the Warner Brothers company bought the Metropolitan and managed it until it was razed in 1968, a final victim to the predominance of television. At the present time, it is a restaurant.

SITE B29: FORD'S THEATER AT 511 TENTH STREET. It was here on April 14, 1865 (about the time this photo was taken), that the 16th president of the United States, Abraham Lincoln, was shot by actor John Wilkes Booth. As part of a conspiracy to avenge the South's surrender at Appomattox one week before, Secretary of State William Seward was also injured. After the assassination, the building was used as government offices and storage space. In 1893, the floor collapsed, killing 22 government workers. It became the Army Medical Museum (now at Walter Reed Medical Center) and continued as government storage through most of the 20th century. In 1968, the building was restored and again served as a theater and museum of Lincoln memorabilia. *Open to the public.*

SITE B30: PETERSEN HOUSE AT 516 TENTH STREET. Directly across from Ford's Theater is the house where Lincoln died. This three-story townhouse was built in 1849 by William Peterson, who rented out the top rooms of the house while working as a tailor on the first floor. After the assassination, Lincoln was carried across the street from Ford's Theater into a small guest room at the back of the first floor. The tenant of this room was a Pauline Petersen Wenzing, who happened to be away at boarding school at the time. Lincoln died there without regaining consciousness in the early morning of April 15, 1865. Later, Petersen sold the house to the Shade family, whose children continued to use the bedroom as their own. The federal government bought the house in 1896, and a museum was established in 1932. It is now a property of the National Park Service. *Open to the public.*

SITE B31: ST. PATRICK'S CATHOLIC CHURCH AT F AND TENTH STREETS. On this site stood a small Catholic wooden chapel built by Fr. Anthony Caffrey in 1796, marking the first established Catholic church in Washington, D.C. It was intended to supply the Irish workers—who were building the Capitol, the White House, and other public buildings—with a suitable place to worship inside the new Federal City. Later, in 1809, a large Gothic-Revival church was built on the southern part of the city block but was razed in 1872. The new structure pictured here was built in 1884 and continues to serve the Catholic community in Washington, D.C. On this site, Christian Hines remembers that "on the square bounded by F and G and Tenth and Eleventh Streets, three frame houses: one was a Presbyterian church or meetinghouse. This and St. Patrick's church were the only public places of worship between Rock Creek and the Capitol."

SITE B32: THE FIRST CONGREGATIONAL CHURCH AT G AND TENTH STREETS NW. In November 1866, the First Congregational Church was formed on this site after two previous attempts failed. It seems that the church's close association with anti-slavery sentiments in a pro-slavery territory prevented the previous attempts to establish a church. Yet after the Union troops occupied the city during the Civil War, an attempt to gather funds from the National Council was finally granted. The leading benefactor in the establishment of the church was Gen. Oliver O. Howard, who headed the Freedman's Bureau and Howard University. The church was built in 1866 and continued to serve its congregation until it was razed for a more modern building in 1959. Christian Hines remembers that the "square bounded by G and H and Ninth and Tenth Streets, one wooden farm-house occupied by Mr. Burns, (brother to Davy Burns, the owner,) with a small orchard to the rear. From this to Boundary [now Florida Avenue], old fields and woods."

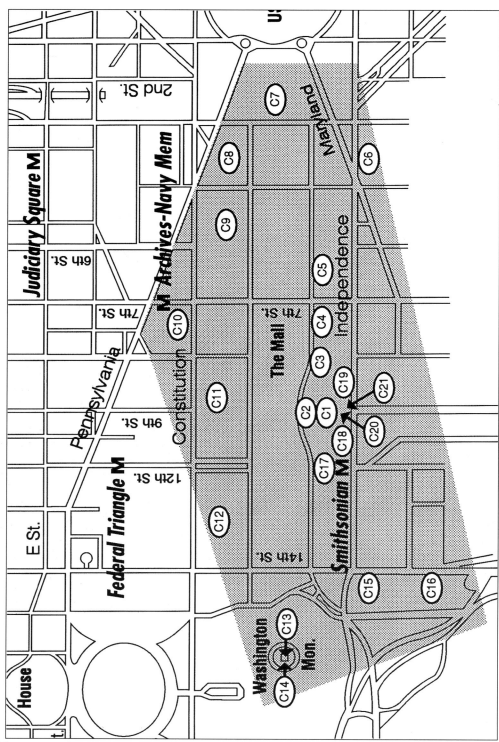

MAP OF THE EAST MALL.

Tour C
THE EAST MALL

In 1790, Washington, D.C., was nearly 5,000 acres of woods, valleys, and pasture land. Pierre L'Enfant was the architect hired by the federal commissioners in 1791 to transform this rustic woodland into a major city by 1800. The centerpiece of his design would be the Mall or, as he called it, "The Grand Avenue."

Under L'Enfant's plan, the Mall was a mile long and 400 feet wide. It began just west of the ellipse near the White House and ended near the foot of the Capitol. The canal, and later a university, were to be in between the mansions and embassies that lined the sides.

For the first 50 years or so, the Mall remained mostly wilderness. The Washington City Canal was the Mall's centerpiece, running, as it did, from Foggy Bottom to Capitol Hill. Congress finally authorized noted landscape architect Andrew Jackson Downing to landscape the Mall in 1850. His design included circular walks, gardens, trees, and plants. In 1931, the Mall was once again redesigned to fit more closely to L'Enfant's original plan. In 1965, the Owings Plan eliminated all vehicular traffic along the Mall to make it a pedestrian park.

Since the early days of Washington, the Mall has been the site of markets, greenhouses, parks, and military parade grounds. Even buffalo roamed the Enid Haupt Gardens, found behind the Smithsonian Castle, as part of the first national zoo in the 1880s. You'll see that military reunions, peace marches, civil rights demonstrations, war protesters, festivals, parades, and memorials of all kinds continue to make the Mall the historic meeting place of the nation.

SITE C1: SMITHSONIAN CASTLE. "To found at Washington, under the name of the Smithsonian Institution, an establishment for the increase and diffusion of knowledge among men." This is the bequest of James Smithson, an English scientist, to the United States—a country he never even visited. The bequest, about $500,000 at today's rate, was conditional: Smithson's nephew must have died without an heir. He did in 1835. In 1846, Congress created the Smithsonian Institution to manage the bequest. The Smithsonian "Castle" was built as the first national museum, but now is the administrative headquarters for all of the Smithsonian museums. It was designed by James Renwick in 1852, with help from Congressman Robert Dale Owen of Indiana, who influenced the design of the Norman castle design and oversaw its construction. The castle is one of the earliest examples of Romanesque-Gothic style in the United States. The Renwick Gallery of Art, Grace Church, and St. Patrick's Cathedral in New York are also Renwick designs. Visit the Information Center inside. The gift shop and historical video should be of interest as well.

SITE C2: JOSEPH HENRY MEMORIAL. The famed scientist who perfected the use of the electromagnet (the unit of measure of induction is called a "Henry") was named the first secretary of the Smithsonian Institution in 1846. Through the next 32 years, Henry would create a legacy distributing original research throughout the world. He established the use of the telegraph to predict weather patterns and storm conditions. His lectures, intended "to give instruction rather than amusement," were very popular and only reluctantly allowed public exhibits of Smithsonian artifacts. This 9-foot bronze statue, with an electromagnet in relief on the pedestal, was designed by William Wetmore Story in 1883 and placed here by an Act of Congress. After Henry's death in 1878, Pres. Rutherford B. Hayes and Congress publicly eulogized Henry while John Philip Sousa conducted *The Transit of Venus March*, written especially for the unveiling.

SITE C3: ARTS AND INDUSTRIES BUILDING. This was the Smithsonian's first museum building. Designed by Adolph Cluss, this Romanesque-style building was completed in 1881 and covers 2.3 acres. The first public use of the building was for Pres. James A. Garfield's Inaugural Ball on March 4, 1881. It was attended by nearly 5,000 guests. The building originally housed the major collections now scattered among the other Smithsonian Buildings, including Charles Lindbergh's *Spirit of St. Louis* airplane and the huge American flag from Fort McHenry that inspired the national anthem. Today, this building houses rotating collections of everyday life.

SITE C4: HIRSHHORN MUSEUM AND SCULPTURE GARDEN. Opened in 1974, the museum houses the "world's biggest personal collection of modern art," once belonging to Joseph H. Hirshhorn (1899–1981). Pres. Lyndon Johnson personally welcomed the donation of such a vast collection for the American people in a White House ceremony on May 17, 1966. The collection includes nearly 2,000 sculptures and nearly 5,000 paintings, drawings, and prints. On this site also stood the Army Medical Museum from 1887 until 1969. Founded in 1862 by Brig. Gen. Alexander Howard, surgeon general during Lincoln's term, the museum occupied several sites around Washington, D.C.—including Ford's Theater—until it moved to this site in 1887. The museum had one of the world's largest collections of medical specimens, publications, books, and artifacts; two examples of these are fragments of Lincoln's skull and the amputated leg of Gen. Daniel Sickles, who killed Francis Scott Key's son in Lafayette Square earlier in his career. See Tour D for more details. The exhibit is now housed at the Walter Reed Hospital, named after the curator of the museum in the 1890s.

SITE C5: NATIONAL AIR AND SPACE MUSEUM. This museum opened on July 4, 1976, the bicentennial of the U.S., with its 200,000 square feet of museum space designed by Gyo Obata. It is considered to be the most heavily visited museum in the world. *Open to the public 10 a.m. to 5:30 p.m. daily.* Here the Washington Armory stood, a small neo-classical structure built in 1855 that was used to store the weapons for the Washington Artillery and the Light Infantry company or local police force until 1865. After the Civil War, the building was the headquarters for the U.S. Fish Commission (now the Fish and Wildlife Service) and government offices before being razed for the Air and Space Museum. This photo shows a series of 50 wooden buildings known as the Armory Square Hospital. Nurses, doctors, and volunteers tended the wounded here during the Civil War. Pres. Abraham Lincoln visited writer Walt Whitman during his convalescence here.

SITE C6: DEPARTMENT OF HEALTH AND HUMAN SERVICES IN THE HUBERT H. HUMPHREY FEDERAL BUILDING. Completed in 1976, this is one of two federal office buildings in Washington, D.C., designed by Marcel Breuer; the other is the Department of Housing and Urban Development building. Humphrey served as mayor of Minneapolis, governor, and influential Democratic senator from Minnesota before becoming Lyndon Johnson's vice president in 1964. After losing the presidential election in 1968 to Richard Nixon, Humphrey returned to the Senate until his death in 1978. The Voice of America radio station is also housed here. Interstate 395 runs directly beneath this building and the Mall as it travels north into Maryland and south into Virginia.

SITE C7: CAPITOL REFLECTING POOL AND THE U.S. CAPITOL. This pool, designed by the firm of Skidmore, Owings & Merrill, was completed in 1970. Interstate 395 runs directly beneath it. The pool beautifully reflects the U.S. Capitol located directly behind. This view is of the West Front, where the presidential inauguration has taken place ever since Ronald Reagan's first inaugural in 1981. It was a spot chosen specifically by Pierre L'Enfant and approved by George Washington because it was 88 feet above the Potomac and afforded a commanding view of the Federal City. The entire Capitol complex occupies 3.5 acres. It is 750 feet long and nearly half as wide. Just in front of the reflecting pool was the fork of the Washington City Canal. From here, it turned south and branched into two separate forks before emptying into the Anacostia River, which is now Canal Street. As early as 1791, L'Enfant had planned a canal through the Federal City as a way to ease the transportation of building materials and supplies to the city. Not until 1810 was the canal finally begun; however, by 1826, merchants were complaining that the canal wasn't deep enough or wide enough. The canal remained difficult to maintain, and traffic continued to decline. Before the 1870s, it became a health hazard and was finally covered. Only the lock house at 17th and Constitution Avenue (the site of the canal itself) remains.

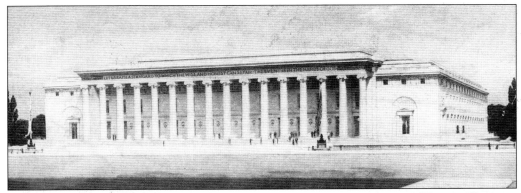

SITE C8: NATIONAL GALLERY OF ART, EAST WING: CONSTITUTION AND FOURTH STREETS NW. I.M. Pei designed this completely modern museum and opened it as an art exhibit itself in 1978. Paul Mellon (1907–99), son of the famous benefactor Andrew Mellon, created the building around his personal collection of modern art. This building is connected underground to the older, more traditional West Wing of the National Gallery of Art. The exhibits of modern art are justifiably enhanced by the triangular shape of the building built on a triangular piece of land. Alexander Calder's naturally shifting mobile *Untitled*, located in the Central Court, is itself worth a visit. The George Washington Victory Memorial Building is seen here in 1914. Only the foundation and cornerstone were laid on November 14, 1921, when this building was dedicated as a museum and archives for American military veterans. Intended as a joint venture with Columbian University, the final funding never materialized, and the foundation was removed for the National Gallery of Art Building. The joint venture did manage to have a lasting impact when Columbian University agreed to change its name to the George Washington University. The Kennedy Center for the Performing Arts nows serves virtually the same purpose and actually looks somewhat similar to the original design of the Memorial Building, with its row of columns along its main facade.

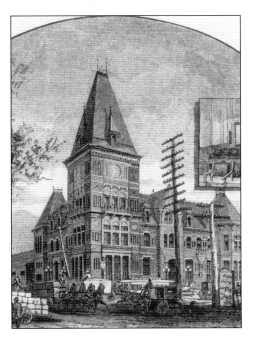

SITE C9: NATIONAL GALLERY OF ART, WEST BUILDING. John Russell Pope designed this neo-Classical building in 1941. Andrew W. Mellon (1855–1937), former secretary of the treasury, contributed not only the building, but also his personal collection of 121 world-class, Old Masters paintings as the nucleus of the collection. Also on this site stood the Tyler House. It was the residence of Vice Pres. John Tyler in 1841 when he was summoned to assume the presidency after the death of Pres. William Henry Harrison. This death occurred one month after Harrison's inauguration. This photo shows the Baltimore and Potomac Railroad Station that stood on this site from 1873 until 1902. The assassination of Pres. James A. Garfield occurred here on September 19, 1881. An additional railroad terminal at New Jersey and C Streets (the Baltimore and Ohio Railroad; see Site A32) was also in operation from 1852 until 1902, when both terminals were demolished and combined into the new Union Station terminal.

SITE C10: NATIONAL ARCHIVES. Throughout most of the early U.S. history, official and historical documents were carted from place to place and stored haphazardly in any cubbyhole or open space. Papers and records were burned by the British during its occupation of Washington in 1814, and numerous fires decimated even more documents. Storehouses were constructed in the early 20th century, but this proved to be an inadequate archival system. Only in 1926 did Congress approve funds for the building of the National Archives, a separate archival and historical research branch. Opened in 1935, the building itself, designed by John Russell Pope (National Gallery of Art, DAR Constitution Hall, Scottish Rite Temple) sits on 8,500 concrete pilings driven 21 feet to bedrock to support the huge structure built on marshy land. Inside the main entrance is the rotunda that exhibits the authentic Declaration of Independence, Bill of Rights, and the Constitution. Special exhibits are always added and changed regularly. *Open to the public 10 a.m. to 5 p.m. during fall and winter, 10 a.m. to 9 p.m. during other seasons. Tours available.*

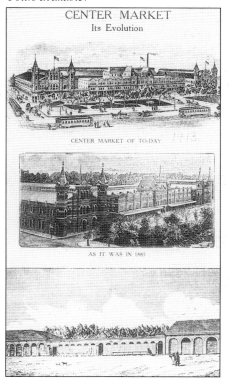

CENTER MARKET
Its Evolution

CENTER MARKET OF TO-DAY

AS IT WAS IN 1885

CENTER MARKET IN 1871. The first outdoor market in Washington was located on Lafayette Square across from the White House as early as 1793. It was mentioned in early newspaper accounts of George Washington's march through the city to lay the cornerstone of the Capitol in 1793. Since the square was then the social and business center of the city, citizen complaints forced its removal to this site in 1801. It was known by the locals as the "Marsh Market" because it was located on marsh land with the canal along its south entrance (now Constitution Avenue). In 1872, Adolph Cluss designed a massive brick structure that housed 1,000 individual stalls, artesian wells, and an ice plant considered to be the most modern and sanitary in the country. Of the five markets operating until the 1920s, only two—Eastern Market at North Carolina and Seventh Streets SE and Northern Market at O Street and Seventh Street NW—remain. Center Market was demolished in 1931 for the construction of the National Archives.

Site C11: National Museum of Natural History. This was the "new" National Museum when it opened in 1911. It was designed by the firm of Hornblower and Marshall, and two additional wings were added in 1965 to house the more than 81 million artifacts, including the famous Hope diamond, a life-size African bush elephant, fossils, petrified logs, mammals, birds, sea creatures, and much more. Just outside the National Museum of American History stands a three-dimensional, stainless-steel sculpture designed by Jose de Rivera depicting Infinity. Completed in 1967, the sculpture is 16 feet long, 13.5 feet high, and 8 feet wide. The sculpture rotates on the black granite base every six minutes. *Open to the public 10 a.m. to 5:30 p.m. daily. Tours available.*

Site C12: National Museum of American History. Originally called the National Museum of History and Technology when it opened in 1964, this museum was created to separate the historical and technological artifacts from the more natural artifacts. The name was changed in 1980 to the National Museum of American History. *Open to the public 10 a.m. to 5:30 p.m. daily.* This photo shows the old Agriculture Department Greenhouses (lower right). These formal gardens and greenhouses of the original Department of Agriculture were located just south of here across the Mall. The formal gardens were designed by William Saunders in 1870 and included terraced flower beds. The greenhouses were razed c. 1940 to accommodate temporary housing for an Army-Air Force unit. The housing was finally razed to make room for the National History Museum in the early 1960s.

SITE C13: WASHINGTON MONUMENT. In 1783, Congress authorized an equestrian statue to the commander-in-chief of the Continental Army during the Revolutionary War, George Washington. It wasn't until 1833 that a private group, the Washington Monument Society, was founded to raise money to erect a fitting memorial. In 1848, the cornerstone was laid. Due to lack of funds, the work halted at 150 feet in 1854 and remained incomplete until Congress finally granted the funds to complete the memorial in 1876. It was finally completed in 1886, 103 years after Congress authorized a monument built on this spot. The Corps of Army Engineers completed this simple obelisk designed by Robert Mills with the 898 steps and 50 landings supported by walls that are 15-feet thick at the base and 18 inches at its 555.5-foot pinnacle. The "water line" at the 152-foot mark is from the use of slightly different stone from the same Maryland quarry. Just southeast of the Washington Monument is an outdoor theater, the National Sylvan Theater, created in 1917 by Congress for use during the summer months for Shakespearean plays and musical concerts.

SITE C14: JEFFERSON PIER. This small stone monument marks the true axis of Pierre L'Enfant's intersection of north-south and east-west where the Capitol and the monument were to balance each other. However, to compensate for the condition of the land, the monument was placed somewhat off the original mark. The original stone was placed here in 1810 and removed sometime later, but it was replaced once again in 1889. Just to the west and south, covering the Lincoln and Jefferson Memorials, was the Potomac River. During heavy rains, the river would actually flood all the way to the ellipse just north of here.

SITE C15: U.S. HOLOCAUST MEMORIAL MUSEUM. This is one of the newest museums in Washington, D.C. Opened in 1993 in a building designed by James Ingo Freed, the museum is dedicated to preserving the memory of the six million people who died at the hands of the Nazi regime in Germany between 1933 and 1945. It is intended "to remember those who suffered, and to inspire visitors to contemplate the moral implications of their choices and responsibilities as citizens in an interdependent world." *Open to the public 10 a.m. to 5:30 p.m. every day. Free tickets are required for the Permanent Exhibit.*

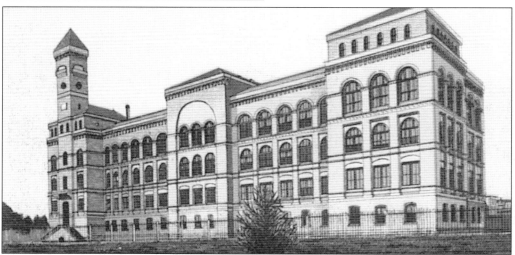

SITE C16: BUREAU OF ENGRAVING AND PRINTING, U.S. TREASURY. This huge complex was occupied in 1914 and encompassed the original building built in 1880. It is here that a visitor will view the printing of U.S. currency, although the Bureau also prints postage stamps, notes, certificates, and other national currencies. The Bureau was begun in 1862 when the first "greenback" was printed. Prior to that, each individual colonial government printed its own currency. *Enter on Fourteenth Street near C Street. Open Mon-Fri 8:30 a.m. to 3:30 p.m. No admission. Tickets required.* On this site stood the Casanave House, owned by Benjamin Young. Young acquired the land holding in the early 18th century from Lord Calvert of Maryland. When his son Notley Young died in 1802, this land was divided between his two daughters, Ann and Eleanor. Ann Casanave, wife of former Georgetown mayor Peter Casanave, built a distinguished home with a sweeping view of meadows and the Potomac River. By the end of the 19th century, the area became very industrialized, and the house was demolished in 1913 for the Bureau of Engraving and Printing.

SITE C17: FREER GALLERY OF ART.

Walking through the Gallery evokes the feel of the Renaissance palace Charles A. Platt designed it to be in 1923. The central courtyard with fountains is restful and very conducive to viewing the collection of Charles Lang Freer (1854–1919), a Detroit Michigan industrialist. Freer was known for his collection of James McNeill Whistler prints, as well as Oriental art and late-19th- and early-20th-century American works. Freer donated his collection to the nation as part of the Smithsonian Institution. Today, the collection contains about 10,000 objects, including Whistler's wonderful Peacock Room. *Open to the public 10 a.m. to 5:30 p.m. Tours available. No admission fee.*

GENERAL NOBLE REDWOOD TREE HOUSE IN 1894. Just on the other side of Twelfth Street and near the west side of the Freer Gallery stood the "oldest" structure in Washington, D.C. In 1894, a rather large section of a 2,000-year-old sequoia tree was placed on the Mall. It was cut in 1892 from the General Grant National Park in California for the World Columbian Exposition in Chicago. The tree measured 85 feet in circumference and was 50 feet high. It had an interior staircase built inside, and visitors could walk to the top to view the Mall from a contemporary-style shingled roof and dormer windows. When the Mall was re-landscaped, the tree was removed to storage in 1932 and disappeared. It was named for Brig. Gen. John Willock Noble, who, as secretary of the interior from 1889 to 1893, preserved millions of acres of western forests from development.

SITE C18: SACKLER GALLERY OF ASIAN ART. Architect John Paul Carlhian had the unique opportunity to create an unusual major art museum complex. By visiting this three-level, 360,000-square-foot museum of Asian art, it is hard to tell that it is located 57 feet underground and below a 4-acre garden! The collection of 1,000 pieces of Asian art was donated by Dr. Arthur M. Sackler (1913–87) with a pledge of $4 million to build a museum to house it. It opened in 1987 to join the Smithsonian Institution family. *Open to the public 10 a.m. to 5:30 p.m. Tours available. No admission fee.*

SITE C19: NATIONAL MUSEUM OF AFRICAN ART. In conjunction with the Sackler Gallery of Asian Art, the Museum of African Art shares similar space. The original collection of purely sub-Saharan African art was donated by Foreign Service officer Warren Robbins and opened along with the Sackler in 1987. Both museums are completely underground. The collection was first housed in the Frederick Douglass townhouse on Capitol Hill beginning in 1964. It became a Smithsonian Institution collection in 1979 and moved here in 1987. On this site also stood Cameron Row, two Greek Revival brick townhouses built by master stonemason Gilbert Cameron. One was his residence, and the other was a rental property. Most early homes in Washington, D.C., were constructed this way. They were finally demolished in 1941, along with other homes, to widen Independence Avenue.

SITE C20: SPENCER FULLERTON BAIRD STATUE. As an American zoologist, Baird published *Catalogue Of North American Mammals* in 1857, *Catalogue of North American Birds* in 1858, and *A History of North American Birds* in 1874. He was the first U.S. Commissioner of Fish and Fisheries and was the second secretary of the Smithsonian Institution when he died in 1877.

SITE C21: ANDREW JACKSON DOWNING URN. One of the pioneer landscape architects of the 1840s, Downing influenced the career of renowned American landscape architect Frederick Law Olmsted through his prolific publications and plant experiments. Downing designed an informal, park-like atmosphere on the Mall in 1850, similar to Central Park in New York, with circular paths and filled with trees and plants. The Mall was redesigned in 1931 to closely resemble L'Enfant's large and open design of 1791. The ellipse and Lafayette Park near the White House are the only original Downing plans left. Still, his influence was important in the 19th century. This decorative 4-foot urn designed by Calvert Vaux was originally placed near the National Museum of Natural History as a memorial to Downing in 1856 after he died in a steamboat accident on the Hudson River at the age of 37 in 1852. The urn was moved to this location in 1972.

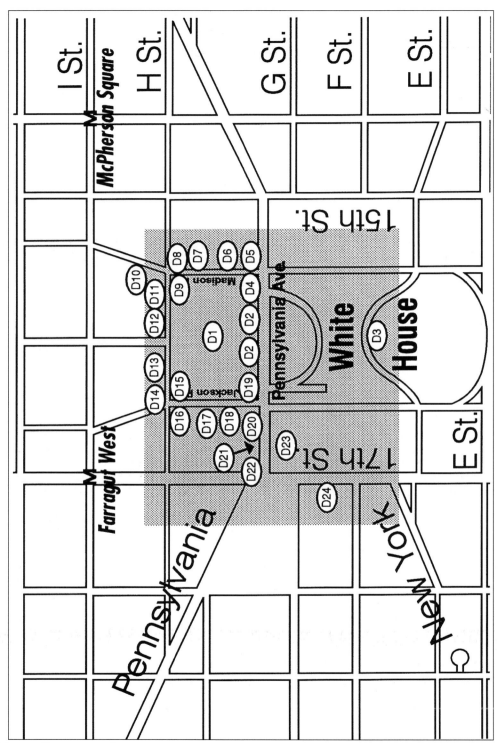

MAP OF LAFAYETTE SQUARE.

Tour D

LAFAYETTE SQUARE

"Lafayette Square was society . . . Beyond the square the country began."
—*Historian and author Henry Adams*

The sentiment of Henry Adams even applies today. But in the late 18th century, the park was an orchard and the site of the Peerce family graveyard. In 1790, Davey Burns reluctantly sold the lot to the Federal City, and it became the north grounds of the President's house.

When it came time to lay the cornerstone for the new Capitol in 1791, George Washington marched through Lafayette Square, passing through the first outdoor market in Washington.

By 1808, Pres. Thomas Jefferson created the square by directing that Pennsylvania Avenue be cut through to create a strictly public park. It immediately became known as President's Park. Later, in 1824, it was renamed Lafayette Park to honor the Revolutionary War patriot Marquis de Lafayette on his visit to the United States.

By 1845, Lafayette Square became the center of social and political life in the new capital. In fact, visitors were kept waiting to see the President in Lafayette Square so often it became known as the "lobby of the White House."

In the 1960s, after decades of neglect, Jacqueline Kennedy successfully campaigned to preserve Lafayette Square's 19th-century heritage from commercial and governmental development. We can now enjoy Lafayette Square's 7 acres of brick walks, classic sculpture, park benches, and 97 varieties of trees. So, come walk the same paths that presidents, statesmen, royalty, and commoners have walked for over 200 years.

SITE D1: STATUE OF GENERAL ANDREW JACKSON. In 1853, this became the first equestrian sculpture cast in the U.S. The sculptor, Clark Mills, melted the British cannons captured by Jackson at the Battle of New Orleans during the War of 1812 for the statue. Mills also sculpted the equestrian statue of George Washington. Located in Washington Circle, it was the first statue of President Washington in the capital. The names of the four 870-pound cannons at the base of the statues are El Egica, El Aristo, El Apolo, and Witiza. Lafayette Square was enclosed by an iron fence shortly after the statue of General Jackson was unveiled in 1853. It remained fenced until 1899 when it was removed and sent to Gettysburg.

SITE D2: THE NAVY YARD URNS. These urns stand on either side of the south entrance to Lafayette Park, but little is known of their creation. They are inscribed "Ordnance Department, US Navy Yard, Washington, DC 1872." They were placed in the park in 1872 by order of Secretary of the Navy George M. Robeson, and the urns originally stood on the east and west side of the Jackson statue. They were relocated here after the park was redesigned in 1936. The urns themselves each stand 5 feet high and 4 feet wide on a base of granite of 6.5 feet high and 4.5 feet wide at the base.

SITE D3: THE WHITE HOUSE. Begun in 1792, Irish architect James Hoban designed the home (depicted in this 1803 watercolor just left of center) with a total of 132 rooms, making this the largest home in America until the Civil War. Its first occupant was Pres. John Adams in 1801.

THE WHITE HOUSE. In August of 1814, the White House was burned by a British occupation force. When it was rebuilt by 1817, the sandstone was painted white, presumably to hide the burn marks. Actually, like today, it was intended as a protective coating. Only since 1903 has the mansion been formally known as the White House. The North Portico that you see was added in 1824; the South Portico was added in 1829. The Truman balcony was added during the complete renovation of 1948. During the minor renovations in 1903, the West Wing (right) was added as offices for the President and staff. The East Wing (left) was added in 1948 as offices for the First Lady. *Located at 1600 Pennsylvania Avenue. Call (202)456-7041. Hours: Tuesday through Saturday, 10 a.m. to 12 noon. No admission charge. Get in line early at the White House Visitors Center at Seventeenth and Pennsylvania (see Department of Commerce) for free tickets.*

SITE D4: STATUE OF GENERAL LAFAYETTE. The statue, after its completion in 1891, was described ". . . not as a statue but a gallery." Designed by the French sculptors Jean Alexandre Joseph Falguiere and Marius Jean Antonin Mercie, the bronze figure of Maj. Gen. de Marquis Marie Jean Paul Roch Yves Gilbert Motier de Lafayette is portrayed as petitioning the French National Assembly for assistance to the Americans in their fight for independence. Two cherubs on the north side are holding hands and pointing to an inscription that reads, "By the Congress, in commemoration of the services rendered by General Lafayette and his compatriots during the struggle for the independence of the United States of America." The entire monument is 36 feet high and 20 feet wide. The statue of Lafayette itself is 8 feet high.

SITE D5: THE TREASURY ANNEX: MADISON PLACE AND PENNSYLVANIA AVENUE, NW. Designed by Cass Gilbert in 1919, this neoclassical work incorporates a similar use of ionic columns to balance the ones utilized in the Treasury Building across the street. On this site stood the Dr. James S. Gunnell House. Gunnell was a well-known Washington dentist and city postmaster under President Martin Van Buren. This is also the site of the Freedman's Savings Bank (shown here), which was the most elegant bank in Washington when it was built in 1869. In the beginning, it served as a bank to protect the savings on various military posts during the Civil War era, and grew to more than 30 branches in many Southern states. Due to internal corruption and inept accounting, the trustees hired noted abolitionist Frederick Douglass as its executive in 1874; unfortunately, the bank went into bankruptcy a few months later. The government bought the building in 1882 and used it for government agencies until it was razed in 1899. The treasury annex was built on the site in 1919.

Site D6: U.S. Court of Claims Building. This modern, red-brick building was built in the 1960s as the headquarters to consolidate the federal claims court system. Visit the courtyard inside. On this site stood the Commodore John Rodgers's House (shown here), built *c.* 1831. It was sold to Secretary of State Seward in 1863. On April 14, 1865, Lewis Paine stabbed Seward in the throat as part of the Lincoln assassination plot. Secretary Seward survived. Paine, Mary Surratt, and the others were later convicted and hanged for their roles in the assassination. John Wilkes Booth, Lincoln's assassin, was killed while escaping to Maryland.

Lafayette Square Opera House and Belasco Theater. Also on this site stood the Washington Club, where in 1859, Philip Barton Key, the son of Francis Scott Key (composer of the national anthem), was murdered by New York Congressman Dan Sickles. Key had been having a secret affair with Sickles's wife, Teresa. Sickles was later acquitted by reason of insanity. This was the first time such a defense was used in the U.S. courts. The house was demolished in 1894 to build the Lafayette Square Opera House, which was later renamed the Belasco Theater (shown here) in 1906. Here Enrico Caruso, Al Jolson, Will Rogers, and Helen Hayes began their careers. It was demolished for the Court of Claims building in 1964.

SITE D7: BENJAMIN OGLE TAYLOE HOUSE AT NO. 21 MADISON PLACE. This house, built in 1828, preserves much of its original architectural charm. The son of Col. John Tayloe of the Octagon House, Benjamin Ogle Tayloe was part of the social history of Washington, D.C., during its first years. Pres. William Henry Harrison was to have visited the house just before he died in 1841. Later, other occupants included Vice Pres. Garrett Hobart and Senator Mark Hanna of Ohio. Hanna was so close to President McKinley, who was also from Ohio, that the house was called "The Little White House." The Cosmos Club purchased the property as part of its expansion in 1917. The house remained part of the club until 1952, when the club moved to 2121 Massachusetts Avenue NW.

SITE D8: CUTTS-MADISON HOUSE. This house was built in 1819 by Dolley Madison's brother-in-law Richard Cutts. Mrs. Madison lived here for 13 years after President Madison's death in 1836. It was Dolley Madison who saved several important White House furnishings (including the large portrait of George Washington that still hangs in the East Room of the White House) before the British captured the city during the War of 1812. During the Civil War, Gen. George McClellan used the house as his headquarters. The house was purchased by the Cosmos Club in 1886, and the third floor and flat roof were immediately added. The club moved to its new headquarters on Massachusetts Avenue in 1952 when the entire club property (21, 23, 25, and 27 Madison Place) were bought by the U.S. government for use as offices.

SITE D9: STATUE OF KOSCIUSKO. This monument to Polish patriot Thaddeus Kosciuszko commemorates a lifetime dedicated to fighting for freedom in America and Poland. In this memorial, a heroic bronze of Kosciuszko stands 8 feet high upon a granite pedestal facing north. He wears the uniform of a general of the Continental Army and holds in his right hand a map of the fortifications at Saratoga. On the east face, a group shows Kosciuszko in American uniform freeing a bound soldier symbolizing the American army. There is a flag in Kosciusko's left hand, and a fallen musket and overturned drum are at the youth's feet. On the west face, a fallen Kosciuszko in Polish uniform attempts to direct a peasant soldier symbolizing the Polish army.

SITE D10: THE DEPARTMENT OF VETERAN AFFAIRS. On this site stood the Arlington Hotel, built in 1868 and enlarged in 1889. It replaced the home of, among others, Sen. Charles Sumner, the New England abolitionist leader. The hotel was said to be the most opulent of the post-Civil War era. Its guests included Prince Albert of Belgium, the Grand Duke Alexis Alexandrovich of Russia, and the Emperor Dom Pedro of Brazil. It was also a permanent home for Speaker of the House Thomas Reed and other members of the Senate and Congress, and it was used as a home away from home for J.P. Morgan and Andrew Carnegie. To keep pace with the times, the old hotel was demolished to make way for a new Arlington Hotel to be built on the same site in 1912. The financing fell through, and the lot instead was sold to the government in 1918 to be used as offices for the newly established Veterans Administration, now the Department of Veterans Affairs.

SITE D11: THE WEBSTER ASHBURTON HOUSE (ST. JOHN'S PARISH HOUSE). This house, built in 1836 by Mathew St. Clair Clark, a former clerk of the House, was later sold to Joseph Gales, editor of the *National Intelligencer*. In 1842, the house was selected by Daniel Webster, then secretary of state, as the residence for the British Minister Alexander Baring, Lord Ashburton. Ashburton's arrival at the house in April 1842 with great quantities of luggage created a "delightful stir," and following the social season "was one of unparalleled gaiety in the history of the first half-century of Washington life. Balls, parties, receptions, and dinners succeeded one another in bewildering rapidity." Both Ashburton and Daniel Webster used entertaining as an extension of their diplomatic duties.

SITE D12: ST. JOHN'S EPISCOPAL CHURCH. This has the distinction of being the first private building on Lafayette Square. It is known as the "Church of the Presidents" because virtually all the Presidents, from James Madison to the present, have worshipped here. Designed by Benjamin Latrobe in 1815, the original central portion of the church was intended to represent a Greek cross with flat dome and a lantern cupola. The church has been enlarged several times over the years, the last addition being the rear nave and several new stained-glass windows in 1883. Pew 54 is traditionally that of the President since it was first bought by President Madison in 1816.

SITE D13: THE HAY-ADAMS HOTEL. The hotel is named for John Hay and Henry Adams, who shared adjoining homes in 1885. John Hay was the private secretary to Pres. Abraham Lincoln as well as the ambassador to Great Britain and later secretary of state under Presidents William McKinley and Theodore Roosevelt. Henry Adams was the grandson of Pres. John Quincy Adams and great-grandson of Pres. John Adams. Adams, a consummate writer of historical work, wrote a nine-volume history of the United States and also biographies of Henry Cabot Lodge, Albert Gallatin, and others. Together, Hay and Adams were the center of social and literary society in Washington throughout the late 19th century. John Hay died in 1905, Henry Adams in 1918.

SITE D14: U.S. CHAMBER OF COMMERCE. This is the kind of massive development that was intended to surround all of Lafayette Square until Jackie Kennedy intervened to preserve the 19th-century facades on either side of the square. This neoclassical structure was built in 1922 by Cass Gilbert on the site of the home of Daniel Webster. Also on this site stood the Slidell House, built in 1845 by banker and bond tradesman William Wilson Corcoran as rental property next to his own. Sen. John Slidell of Louisiana occupied the house from 1853 to 1861. Slidell was elected to the Senate in 1852 but resigned in 1861 to become a diplomat for the Confederate government, unsuccessfully seeking recognition overseas. Slidell remained in Europe after the war and died there in 1871. Corcoran House (shown here), built in 1828, was considered to be the best example of Renaissance Revival architecture in Washington. The house absorbed a house owned by Daniel Webster when it was remodeled in 1849. Both the house and the subsequent Renwick Gallery of Art at 17th Street were designed by architect James Renwick Jr. The Corcoran House was razed in 1922 to make way for the Chamber of Commerce headquarters building.

SITE D15: STATUE OF BARON VON STEUBEN. Baron Friedreich Wilhelm von Steuben spoke no English when he arrived in Valley Forge, Pennsylvania, on February 23, 1778, with a letter of introduction from Benjamin Franklin. He eventually would be universally recognized for turning raw American recruits into a fighting force equal to British regulars. This memorial portrays von Steuben wearing the uniform of a major general of the Continental Army. On the southwest face, *Commemoration* symbolizes a grateful America honoring Steuben. This monument was dedicated on December 7, 1910 (shown above), by Pres. William Howard Taft.

SITE D16: DECATUR HOUSE. This house was built in 1818 by Benjamin Latrobe for Comm. Stephen Decatur. Decatur was the American naval hero who used his prize money won by his victories over the Barbary Pirates (by sinking the captured man o' war ship *Philadelphia* taken captive by the Bey and the British in the War of 1812) to build the first private house on the President's Square. The house was restored to Latrobe's design in 1944. Decatur was killed by Comm. James Barron on the dueling grounds of Bladensburg, Maryland, in 1820. Sometime after his death, his wife sold the property, and it became the embassies of Great Britain, France, and Russia. Vice Pres. George Mifflin Dallas (under James K. Polk), Senator Henry Clay, Secretary of State Martin Van Buren, and others made the Decatur House home. In 1956, the house was bought and restored by the National Trust for Historic Preservation. Today it is maintained as a museum and conference center complex. *Open to the public.*

SITE D17: 736 JACKSON PLACE. Inhabitants here included Franklin Pierce's secretary of state, William Marcy (1853); James G. Blaine, the Republican "Man from Maine" who served in the House, Senate, and in Republican cabinets, but never managed to become president; and Pres. Teddy Roosevelt. The President and his family lived here during the renovation of the White House in 1902. While in residence here, Roosevelt slipped on the front steps and fractured his leg. Next door, at 730 Jackson Place, was the home of Congressman Daniel Sickles. Sickles murdered District Attorney Philip Barton Key in 1859 in Lafayette Park after discovering the young lawyer was having an affair with his wife, Teresa. The scandal rocked Washington, D.C., and led to one of the greatest murder trials in the city's history. Sickles was later acquitted in the killing, marking the first use of the temporary insanity defense in the country. This building was also the first headquarters for the Brookings Institution.

SITE D18: 722 JACKSON PLACE. Built in 1820 but no longer extant, the mansion shown here served as the home to Elihu Root, secretary of war to President McKinley in 1881, and William Randolph Hearst, former Congressman from New York. Nearby, at 712 Jackson Place, was the home of Maj. Henry R. Rathbone, military medical aide to President Lincoln. At the last minute, Major Rathbone replaced Gen. U.S. Grant and his wife as Lincoln's guests to Ford's Theater on the evening of April 14, 1865.

SITE D19: STATUE OF COMTE ROCHAMBEAU. This sculptural group memorializes the arrival of the Comte Jean Baptiste Donatien de Vineur de Rochambeau in America in 1780 as commander of the 5,500-man Royal French Expeditionary Force. He is shown in the uniform of a major general of the Continental Army directing his forces. In his left hand is a plan of battle. At his feet, on the south pedestal face, a bronze group symbolizes France coming to the aid of America. Liberty grasps two flags in her left hand and sword in her right hand as she prepares to defend an embattled eagle symbolizing America. The eagle grasps a shield with 13 stars representing the original colonies. On the west face is the coat of arms of the de Rochambeau family. The monument is a copy of one at de Rochambeau's birthplace in Vendome, France. It was erected by Congress and dedicated by Teddy Roosevelt in 1902.

PEERCE FAMILY GRAVEYARD. On this site, according to Christian Hines, was the Peerce family graveyard. The drawing is a representation of a typical 18th-century graveyard. "[S]ituated on the north side of Pennsylvania Avenue, opposite the President's House, between the southwest corner and south gate of Lafayette Square. Part of it, I think, is covered by the brick pavement that lies along the south side of the square. Peerce's graveyard . . . was situated on tolerably high ground . . . and the graves were all placed in regular order. It appeared to me, when I first saw it, to have been formerly enclosed with a railing . . . and believe it was about thirty-feet square. Previous to putting an iron railing around the square Mr. Harkness, Commissioner of the First ward received orders to graduate and level the square, street, etc. After gathering the remains together and putting them into [a] case, we had them placed in a cart and proceeded to Holmead burying ground [now 20th and Florida Avenue] where we deposited them."

SITE D20: BLAIR HOUSE AT 1651 PENNSYLVANIA AVENUE NW. Surgeon General Joseph Lovell built this house in 1824. In 1837, it was bought by Francis Preston Blair, editor of the *Globe* newspaper. It was at Blair House that Gen. Robert E. Lee declined to head the Union Armies during the Civil War and instead commanded the Confederate forces. Blair House was bought by the federal government as the guest house of the President in 1942 and is now a complex of buildings that includes the Phillips Lee House next door. Here, on November 1, 1950, at 2:15 p.m., Oscar Collazo and Grizelio Torresola, Puerto Rican independence activists, attempted to storm Blair House and assassinate Pres. Harry S. Truman. Truman had been staying here due to White House renovations. In the attempt, several Secret Service agents were wounded, and uniformed officer Leslie Coffelt was killed, but only after he killed Torresola. Collazo survived and was sentenced to death; President Truman reduced the sentence to life imprisonment.

SITE D21: PHILLIPS LEE HOUSE AT 1653 PENNSYLVANIA AVENUE NW. This house, built by Adm. Samuel Phillips Lee in 1859, was a gift to his wife Elizabeth, the daughter of his neighbor Preston Blair. Andrew Johnson lived in the house while serving as vice president under Abraham Lincoln.

SITE D22: THE RENWICK GALLERY. This was the original Corcoran Gallery of Art. It was intended to house the large collection of art belonging to philanthropist William Wilson Corcoran. Completed in 1861, the gallery was immediately seized by the government for use as a temporary hospital and then as headquarters for the Quartermaster General's Corps. In 1869, the gallery was returned to Corcoran, who immediately established the Corcoran Gallery of Art. In 1897, the Corcoran Gallery of Art moved to its present location on Seventeenth Street and donated this building to the federal government. The building housed the U.S. Court of Claims until it was turned over to the Smithsonian to showcase American decorative arts in 1965. Opened to the public in 1972, it was named the Renwick Gallery to honor James Renwick for its design.

SITE D23: THE OLD EXECUTIVE OFFICE BUILDING. This building housed the executive departments of State, War, Navy, and Treasury when it was ordered constructed in 1871 by Pres. U.S. Grant. Construction continued at a slow pace, and it was not completed until 1886. On the site stood the original Executive Office Building, which easily housed all the cabinet departments, when it was completed in 1800. Mocked as the "wedding cake building," it nevertheless is considered the nation's best example of the French Second Empire style. The "OEOB" (as it is affectionately called) has survived countless attempts to have it demolished. It now houses offices for the President's staff and is the official office of the Vice President. *Call (202)3955895. Enter at the Visitors Entrance on Fifteenth Street. Tours are from 9 a.m. to noon Saturday by advance reservation only.*

SITE D24: THE WINDER BUILDING. Built in 1848, this building was named for Gen. William Winder, the defender of Bladensburg, Maryland, during the War of 1812 and defender of Washington, D.C. At five stories tall, it was the first high-rise office building in D.C. It was bought by the U.S. government in 1852 and, during the Civil War, was the headquarters for the U.S. Army. Generals Winfield Scott, U.S. Grant, and others had their headquarters here. Abraham Lincoln reviewed dispatches from the front and visited with Confederate prisoners jailed in the basement. It is now the offices of the U.S. Trade Representative. *Not open to the public.*

Left: **PRESIDENT ABRAHAM LINCOLN.** *Right:* **GENERAL ULYSSES S. GRANT.**

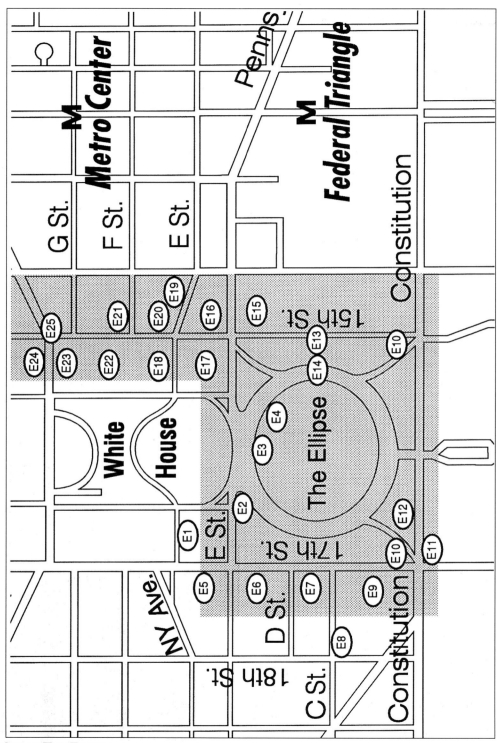

MAP OF THE ELLIPSE.

Tour E

THE ELLIPSE

Tiber Creek flowed just above present-day Constitution Avenue with the Washington Canal being dug just inside and south of the creek. But essentially, this area south of the White House remained virtually undeveloped until the late 19th century. With the Washington Canal south, at the foot of Seventeenth Street came Carbery's Wharf, built at the end of the War of 1812 by Capt. Thomas Carbery. This wharf became the main landing for the building materials intended for the White House and other government buildings throughout Washington, D.C. It was also a main landing point for passenger steamers arriving from Alexandria.

The present design was completed in 1884 as an oval park. Named the Ellipse for its circular roadway on the south side of the White House, it also is sometimes referred to as President's Park South.

SITE E1: FIRST DIVISION MONUMENT. This monument commemorates the sacrifice of 5,599 soldiers of the U.S. Army's First Division of the American Expeditionary Force sent to Europe during WW I. The winged, gilded bronze statue of Victory stands 15 feet tall atop a pink, 65-foot-high granite column, one of the largest single pieces of pink granite ever quarried. Sculptor Daniel Chester French suggested the perfection of the body and soul through the figure's wings while they extend a blessing to the dead. Pres. Calvin Coolidge gave the dedication address on October 4, 1924, to more than 6,000 veterans, Gen. John Pershing, and other military dignitaries. In the summer, the Big Red One, the unit insignia in front of the memorial, is planted with a variety of red flowers.

SITE E2: BUTTMILLETT MEMORIAL FOUNTAIN. This fountain is dedicated to the memory of Maj. Archibald Wallingham Butt and Francis Davis Millet, two well-known members of Washington's social circles of the late-Victorian era. Both friends, Francis Millet was a journalist and artist, and Archibald Butt was an influential military aide to Presidents William Howard Taft and Theodore Roosevelt. Millet was en route to Rome on business at the American Academy and Butt had spent a restful six weeks leave from the White House when both became casualties of the sinking of the *Titanic* on April 14, 1912. The center of this 8-foot fountain was made from a neo-Classical marble shaft and an octagonal base of Tennessee marble. On the south is a military figure representing Military Valor, a reference to Butt's service during the Spanish-American War. The north side contains a figure of an artist with palette and brush representing Art, a reference to Millet's work as a decorative artist and muralist. The memorial was erected entirely from the contributions of friends.

A TITANIC MEMORIAL. An additional *Titanic* memorial is located at Fourth and P Streets SW, across the channel from East Potomac Park. The 18-foot-high granite figure, sculpted by Gertrude Vanderbilt Whitney, represents Self Sacrifice as it memorializes the more than 1,500 people who perished in the sinking of the British steamship *Titanic* on April 15, 1912. Ironically, Mrs. Whitney lost a brother aboard the *Lusitania* when it was sunk by a German submarine on May 7, 1915.

SITE E3: THE ZERO MILESTONE. Sculpted by Horace W. Peaslee, this milestone marks the official point where all distances within the U.S. to and from D.C. are determined.

SITE E4: THE NATIONAL CHRISTMAS TREE. A live, 38-foot Colorado blue spruce from Pennsylvania has been decorated with lights and bulbs every year since 1978. Beginning in 1923 with Calvin Coolidge, the lighting of a national tree has been a holiday tradition, except in 1979 and 1980. In those two years, on orders from Pres. Jimmy Carter, the tree was left unlit as a reminder that 52 Americans were being held hostage in Iran. Since 1954, the tree has been located at its present site. Before then, it was located at several different sites around the White House grounds. Adjacent to the National Christmas Tree, the Christmas Pageant of Peace expands the holiday tradition by providing 57 smaller trees to represent each state, territory, and commonwealth of the United States. There are also live reindeer, a burning Yule log, a Nativity scene, and hot apple cider.

SITE E5: CORCORAN GALLERY OF ART. This is actually the second building to house the collection of millionaire banker William Wilson Corcoran (1798–1888), the man considered to be "Washington's First Philanthropist." As a patron of American art, he installed his collection in the original building located at Seventeenth and Pennsylvania, now known as the Renwick Gallery, when he established the collection in 1869. The current Renaissance Revival building has housed the collection since it was built specifically for the collection in 1897. Both imposing lions on either side of the main entrance are bronze copies of two marble pairs housed at St. Peter's in Rome. It was Italian sculptor Antonio Canova who created the original lions as a memorial for Pope Clement XIII in 1792. Originally, the two bronze lions stood at the entrance to the home of multimillionaire businessman Benjamin Holladay in 1860. After his death in 1888, the lions were bought from his estate and erected on the steps of the original Corcoran Gallery, until the Gallery moved in 1897. *Corner of Seventeenth Street and Pennsylvania Avenue. Call (202)638-3211. Hours: everyday 10 a.m. to 5 p.m; Closed Tuesday; Open Thursday 10 a.m. to 9 p.m. Admission fee required.*

SITE E6: THE RED CROSS HEADQUARTERS. This building was dedicated on October 1, 1953, by Pres. Dwight D. Eisenhower, with the cornerstone having been laid by Pres. Harry Truman in July 1951. The Red Cross is the official agency declared by Congress to oversee national and international emergency and disaster relief as well as to manage the national blood bank program. Its membership doubled to 15 million in WW I and to nearly 36 million during WW II. Today, the Red Cross manages national training in first aid and disaster relief services and is financed by voluntary contributions. Inside the main building on the second-floor conference room is the beautiful *Three Memorial Windows*, a three-paneled, stained-glass window from Tiffany. There are no organized tours. *Open Monday through Friday from 9 a.m. to 5 p.m.*

SITE E7: DAUGHTERS OF THE AMERICAN REVOLUTION AT SEVENTEENTH STREET AND NEW YORK AVENUE. This is part of the original Memorial Constitution Hall built in 1903. It was reopened after renovations in October 1929. Designed by John Russell Pope, the building houses a 4,000-seat auditorium, a museum, and offices for the National Society of the Daughters of the American Revolution. In 1939, Marian Anderson, the world-famous African-American contralto, was denied a concert at Constitution Hall because of her race. Instead, her concert at the Lincoln Memorial was televised nationwide and helped begin the long struggle for civil rights. *Call (202)879-3240. Hours: 8:30 a.m. to 4:00 p.m. Monday through Friday, 1 p.m. to 5 p.m. Sunday, closed Saturday. Free admission.* Also on this site stood the Carbery House, the home of Thomas Carbery, owner of Carbery Wharf, originally located at the foot of Seventeenth Street. Built in 1818, the Carbery House remained on the site until it was demolished to construct the DAR building in 1903. Carbery was a one-time mayor of Washington and a justice of the peace for 40 years.

SITE E8: THE VAN NESS CARRIAGE HOUSE AT EIGHTEENTH AND C STREETS. This one-time outbuilding served as a carriage house for the main Van Ness mansion, built on this site in 1818. Today, it is a storage facility for the Organization of American States.

SITE E9: ORGANIZATION OF AMERICAN STATES (OAS). The OAS is made up of all countries in the Americas and was first founded as the Pan American Union in 1889 and renamed the Organization of American States in 1948. The group's common purpose is to preserve peace, freedom, and welfare for all the people in the western hemisphere. On this site once stood the cottage of Davy Burnes, pictured here. Built in 1750, the one-and-a-half-story wooden building was the main house belonging to Burnes, owner of 527 acres of tobacco land extending from H Street to Constitution Avenue and including most of the land between Third and Eighteenth Streets. The original land grant was bought by David Burnes I in 1721 and included most of the present-day downtown Washington, D.C. Burnes's daughter Marcia Burnes Van Ness, who lived nearby (see below), preserved the cottage throughout her life. It was finally damaged by a storm and razed in 1894.

THE VAN NESS MANSION. Marcia Burnes and her husband, New York Congressman John Peter Van Ness, lived happily here in what was one of the finest homes in Washington when it was completed in 1816. The mansion was built adjacent to Mrs. Van Ness's childhood home known as Burnes cottage. The architect of the Van Ness mansion was Benjamin Latrobe, who also built the White House, Capitol, and Octagon House. After Mrs. Van Ness died in 1846, the mansion became home to newspaper editor Thomas Green. It alternately became home to a German beer garden, a florist nursery, the Columbia Athletic Club, and George Washington University before finally being sold to the federal government in 1907. It was razed to build the OAS (Pan American) building.

SITE E10: FIRST BULFINCH GATEHOUSE. Originally at the entrance of the Capitol from the time it was built in 1828 until 1874, this gatehouse, along with its twin at the other end of the Ellipse at Seventeenth and Constitution, was moved to its present site in 1880. Charles Bulfinch was the first native-born professional architect in the United States. He, along with Benjamin Latrobe, was responsible for rebuilding the Capitol after the British burned it in 1814. The high water marks that can be seen date from 1880 and 1881.

SITE E11: THE LOCK KEEPERS HOUSE. This structure has been located directly across from Constitution Avenue and Seventeenth Street since it was built in the 1830s. Since this was one of the main crossing points between the C&O canal and Tiber Creek, the house served as an inspection station and transfer point. In the early 1870s, the canal was considered a health hazard and was covered, thereby creating Constitution Avenue. This lock keepers house is the only remaining structure from the days of the canal and is maintained as a historic site by the National Park Service. Carefully put your toe over the curb of Constitution Avenue and you would have slid into the Washington Canal, once one of the earliest means of transportation in Washington, D.C. By 1870, it had become an eyesore and was filled in.

SITE E12: SECOND DIVISION MEMORIAL. Built to honor the sacrifice of 17,669 U.S. Army soldiers who died while serving in the Second Division in three wars: WW I, WW II, and the Korean Conflict, the memorial's 18-foot-tall gilded bronze sword symbolically blocks the German Army from entering Paris. The unit insignia, the head of an Indian Chief on a star, is carved in bas relief on the hilt of the sword. Some 250 tons of granite were used to construct the center memorial. Two carved wreaths flank the main section. Originally dedicated by Pres. Franklin D. Roosevelt in 1936, the memorial addition of two outer wings with flagpoles was rededicated by Gen. Maxwell Taylor at a reunion of the Second Division in 1962.

SITE E13: SETTLERS OF THE DISTRICT OF COLUMBIA STONE. This stone is dedicated to the original owners of the land grants (prior to 1700) that make up the present-day Washington, D.C. The 18 landowners whose names are carved below in bas reliefs of corn, tobacco, turkey, and herring—symbols of plenty found in the area—are simply represented by sculptor Carl Mose in this 3-square-foot monument. The National Society of the Daughters of the American Revolution donated this monument in April 1936, believing that it is "a way of teaching history."

SITE E14: BOY SCOUT MEMORIAL.
Dedicated in 1964, this memorial sits on the site of the First National Boy Scout Jamboree in Washington in 1937. The allegorical figures of American Manhood and Womanhood dwarf the representation of the boy scout marching confidently into the future. The boy scout oath is carved on the side of the pedestal that faces the elliptical pool.

SITE E15: THE DEPARTMENT OF COMMERCE. When it was dedicated in 1934, this was the largest office building in the world, covering 8 acres and housing nearly 5,000 federal workers. It has since dropped to third place behind the Pentagon and the Ronald Reagan International Trade Center. This photo shows the original Commerce Department at New Jersey Avenue. At Pennsylvania Avenue and E Street is the entrance to the White House Visitors Center. The Aquarium is also located here with an entrance on Sixteenth Street. On this site stood the Manassas Panorama Building. It was a 16-sided structure built in 1885 that boasted an enormous painted canvas mural of the Second Battle of Manassas, then in 1888, the Battle of Shiloh, and lastly, in 1892, the Battle of Gettysburg. Only the Gettysburg Mural survives. All of the buildings were torn down in 1928 for the Department of Commerce.

SITE E16: PERSHING PARK. This memorial was dedicated to WW I General of the Armies John J. Pershing, commander of the First Division in 1981. The Pershing Victory Arch was erected nearby at Fifteenth Street and Pennsylvania Avenue to welcome home 25,000 WW I troops from France in September 1919. The arch, intended as a patriotic gesture, stayed in place only for a few weeks. Formerly on this site, from 1884 to 1928, was the Albaugh Opera House. The Washington Light Infantry, precursor to the District of Columbia National Guard, had their brick headquarters located here with the opera house occupying the upper-floor, providing rental income for the militia unit. John W. Albaugh was the manager of the Belasco Theatre on Lafayette Square where Helen Hayes got her start. Also located here was the Capital Bicycle Club. Free lessons were provided—and necessary—for the new-fangled contraption. A front tire was over 6 feet tall, but the back tire was only about 2 feet tall. It was an ungainly, dangerous, and very expensive pastime.

SITE E17: GEN. WILLIAM TECUMSEH SHERMAN MONUMENT. Some consider this a monument to peace, Sherman's original objective, while others consider it a monument to the glorification of a cruel military leader. Much has been written on Sherman's march through Atlanta to the Atlantic at Savannah, Georgia, burning everything in sight in order to keep anything useful from returning Confederate troops. Still, Sherman believed that "War's legitimate object is more perfect peace." On the spot where this elaborate statue sits, legend says, is the spot where Sherman stood to review returning Union troops in 1865. The monument, sculpted mainly by Carl RohlSmith and dedicated in 1903, shows Sherman atop his horse 14 feet high, with his field glass in his right hand and his left grasping the reins as if ready for immediate action.

SITE E18: STATUE OF ALEXANDER HAMILTON. Hamilton was the first secretary of the treasury (from 1789 to 1795) and is credited with placing the economy on a sound fiscal basis. For years, a statue to Hamilton was blocked or delayed, but finally, after nearly 100 years, it was unveiled by President Calvin Coolidge (shown here) in 1923. This statue is considered one of the best in a series of memorials by sculptor Augustus SaintGaudens. Hamilton is a bronze sculpture, measuring 10 feet high. He carries a l ng dress coat in one hand and a tricornered hat in the other. The inscription reads "He smote the rock of the national resources and abundant streams of revenue gushed forth. He touched the dead corpse of the public credit and it sprang upon its feet." The donor of the memorial remains anonymous, although newspapers of the time believe it was a mysterious veiled woman.

SITE E29: THE WILLARD-INTERCONTINENTAL HOTEL. This is one of a succession of hotels that has stood on this same site since the Fuller Hotel in 1818. The City Hotel existed from 1840 to 1850, then the Willard brothers built this hotel on the same site. Since 1850, the brothers continuously rebuilt it, enlarging it each time and always calling it the new Willard. Vice Presidents have made it their home, as have senators, foreign legations, and royalty. This would now be the new, new Willard. Treaties have been signed here, and "The Battle Hymn of the Republic" was even penned here. By the time of the 1980s, however, the building was in serious disrepair. It was finally bought, after being vacant for some time, and renovated into its current Victorian style.

Site E20: The Hotel Washington at Fifteenth Street and Pennsylvania Avenue.
The classic ten-story hotel you see today was built around 1917 after the Corcoran Office Building was demolished (far left). Vice Pres. John Nance Garner, Franklin Roosevelt's first VP, made his home here. It was approximately at this site that Maj. Gen. Robert Ross and Rear Adm. George Cockburn stopped at a low brick boardinghouse to have Mrs. Suter prepare a later supper for them since they were on their way to burn the White House. On the extreme left of the photo is the Corcoran Office Building, where the Hotel Washington is now. Along Fifteenth Street stood a series of rowhouses built about 1800 to cater to the new federal government employees in and around the White House. In 1847, William Wilson Corcoran (benefactor of the Corcoran Gallery) razed one of the rowhouses on this corner to erect the first commercial office building in this area. The five-story brick building was razed in 1875 for a larger building nearly twice its size. This newer building took up the entire block of Fifteenth Street from Pennsylvania Avenue to F Street. During the Victorian Era of the late-19th and early-20th century, the building became a haven for the artists of Washington, D.C. The building was razed in 1917 for the Hotel Washington.

SITE E21: GALT & BROS. JEWELERS. Owned by the venerable Galt family of Washington, this preeminent jewelry and silver shop began in 1802. The original location, as pictured here, was between Pennsylvania Avenue and Eleventh and Twelfth Streets and was bought by Norman Galt in 1890 after the death of his father. Norman married Edith Bolling around 1894, and, after his death in 1902, she inherited the jewelry store, debts and all. Later, she was introduced to Woodrow Wilson, and they were married in the White House in 1903. Visit the clock in the lobby that dates to 1836 and the original glass counters dating from 1867 that were in the original store on Pennsylvania Avenue and Eleventh Street.

RHODES TAVERN. On the far right of the photo and under the canopy is what was once known as the "Little Hotel," called that to distinguish it from the "Great Hotel," which referred to Blodgett's Hotel located on E and Eighth Streets from 1793 to 1836. The "Little Hotel" was located at F and Fifteenth Streets and is now the main display area of Galt & Bros. Jewelers. Built in 1801, the hotel was considered to be the first city hall of Washington, D.C., and was once claimed to have been used by British officers during the burning of the White House in 1814. This claim has since been disproved by author Anthony Pitch. The building was razed in 1986 by the Oliver Carr Company for the current structure, despite desperate attempts to save it by preservation groups and citizen outcries. At the time, it was considered the oldest commercial building in Washington, D.C.

SITE E22: U.S. TREASURY BUILDING. This oldest federal building in Washington, D.C. (after the White House and the Capitol), was completed in 1842 after the original building of 1798 and its successor in 1833 both burned to the ground. Christian Hines remembers a fire in the original Treasury building in 1800: "When the alarm of fire was given, several brothers and myself ran up F street to where the fire was. We were informed that the President [John Adams] was in line and busy in aiding to pass the buckets to and from the burning building . . . He did not remain there long, however, for he was advised to withdraw for fear he might take cold." Congress had appropriated money for a new Treasury building in 1833, but could not agree on a site. It is popular legend that impatient old Andrew Jackson rushed out of the White House, thrust his cane into the ground at the northeast corner of the present building, and said to the architect, "Put the cornerstone here, put it right here!" In the Greek Revival style, this building is constructed around an inner court. It is open for tours on Saturdays by appointment only.

SITE E23: STATUE OF ALBERT GALLATIN. This statue faces Pennsylvania Avenue and is said to have been erected to counterbalance the statue of Alexander Hamilton on the south patio. As good as Hamilton was in raising revenue, he still left a $14 million debt after leaving the Treasury in 1801. Gallatin paid it off and even managed to create a surplus before he left the Treasury in 1814. The statue was dedicated October 15, 1947, nearly 20 years after Congressional approval. Gallatin became ambassador to France and Great Britain and, from 1832 to 1839, served as president of the National Bank of New York. He died in 1849. On this site also stood the original Department of State offices. In identical but separate small brick buildings, since 1798, the Treasury occupied the southeast quadrant while the State occupied the northeast quadrant. The State remained here until it was moved into the Old Executive Office Building in 1866. The Treasury building, just behind it, was simply extended to Pennsylvania Avenue.

SITE E24: RIGGS BANK BUILDING. Since 1820, this building (you can see it more clearly on the back of a $10 bill) has occupied the site as a bank. Beginning as a branch of the Second Bank of the U.S., it became a branch bank of the Corcoran and Riggs Bank in 1845 after the Second Bank went bankrupt in 1838. A profitable bank from the beginning, thanks to the federal funds deposited by President Jackson, the bank became Riggs and Company in 1881, then Riggs National Bank in 1896. The adjacent site, now a Nations Bank, was sold to the American Security and Trust Company as the site for its new national headquarters in 1904.

SITE E25: THE FIFTEENTH STREET BEND. This is where the invading British Army, under Maj. Gen. Robert Ross and Rear Adm. George Cockburn, turned to march toward the White House and continue their occupation of Washington, D.C., by burning all public buildings on August 14, 1814. At this corner stood the resplendent Pershing Victory Arch. At the corner of Fifteenth Street and Pennsylvania Avenue stood a large, two-story arch erected to commemorate the WW I homecoming of the U.S. Army First Division led by Gen. John J. Pershing. In September 1919, 15 bands and 25,000 troops marched for four hours in a 5-mile-long procession in front of 400,000 spectators and under the arch. It was dismantled a few weeks later.

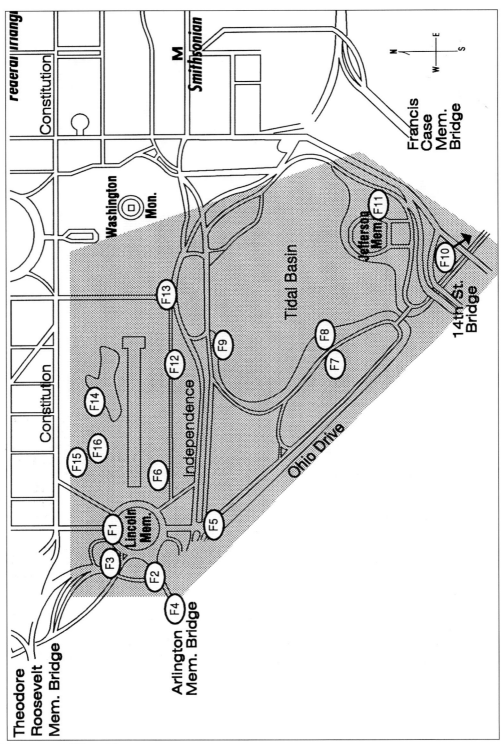

MAP OF THE WEST MALL.

Tour F

THE WEST MALL

"I'll never let a memorial to Abraham Lincoln be erected in that damned swamp."

—*Speaker of the House "Uncle Joe" Cannon*

The reason why Speaker Cannon was so incensed at locating the Lincoln Memorial here was that the West Mall was a muddy mess on its best day. Until the Army Corps of Engineers, between 1880 and 1900, dredged this area and filled it in, it was a fetid, marshy area where wild ducks and turtles made their homes. Christian Hines remembers that "a flat-bottomed boat, at high tide, could be floated up as far as opposite the President's House [the Ellipse]." For most of its early history, the West Mall along Constitution Avenue was essentially a port where ships would unload cargo and canal boats would enter the Washington City Canal.

The 1902 McMillan Plan called for redeveloping the capital city "as a work of civic art." The West Mall would provide the location for a Lincoln Memorial and a Hall of the Founding Fathers (this was later replaced by a memorial to Thomas Jefferson). The plan also included playing fields, parks filled with trees near the Lincoln Memorial, and beaches with gardens near the Tidal Basin. The beaches disappeared, but the monuments remain.

Today, the area known as the West Mall is one of the most visited areas of Washington, D.C. Built as a type of "breakwall" to prevent flooding along the Mall, East Potomac Park was created in the late 1880s. Hains Point, at the very tip of the park, memorializes the efforts of Maj. Gen. Peter C. Hains, who successfully completed this project for the Army Corps of Engineers.

SITE F1: LINCOLN MEMORIAL. "In this Temple, as in the hearts of the people, for whom he saved the union, the memory of Abraham Lincoln is enshrined forever." These are the words carved on the 14-foot-high Indiana limestone wall just behind Lincoln's head as sculpted by Daniel Chester French. The marble stonework is made from 28 blocks of Georgia marble and took four years to complete. The memorial, designed by Henry Bacon, is in a Greek Temple style. The entire memorial sits on pilings drilled into bedrock 44 to 65 feet below ground. Around the perimeter of the memorial are 36 white marble, Greek Doric columns representing the number of states in the Union at the time of Lincoln's death. They are each 44 feet high and 7.5 feet in diameter and were designed to tilt inward, thereby making the rounded roofline less prominent. The 48 seals around the frieze represent the states in the Union when the memorial was dedicated (with Lincoln's son Robert Todd in attendance) on May 30, 1922. The Reflecting Pool is almost 2,000 feet long, nearly 1/3 of a mile long, and holds almost 25,000 gallons of water. Since its dedication in 1922, the Lincoln Memorial has been host to several historic events. On Easter Sunday in 1939, Marian Anderson sang from the steps in front of 75,000 people. This happened after she had been barred from Constitution Hall, run

by the Daughters of the American Revolution, due to her African-American heritage. First Lady Eleanor Roosevelt protested the decision, resigned from the organization, and had the concert moved here. Nearly 25 years later, in 1963, the Reverend Martin Luther King delivered his "I Have A Dream" speech in front of 250,000 Freedom Marchers at the foot of the Lincoln Memorial. See the small museum at the foot of the stairs to your right for a history of the construction of the memorial and its place in the history of the civil rights movement.

DANIEL CHESTER FRENCH.

SITES F2 AND F3: "THE ARTS OF WAR" AND "THE ARTS OF PEACE." At the entrance to Arlington Memorial Bridge stand two gilded bronze sculptures by Leo Friedlander depicting the "defensive power of the Nation" as represented by the male Mars astride a horse. The standing female with the shield represents Valor; the other female represents Sacrifice. The statue was originally commissioned in 1925, but due to funding, WW II, and other considerations, it was finally completed by the government of Italy as a token of understanding between the two countries. It was dedicated in 1951. The second sculpture grouping, "The Arts of Peace," stands at the entrance to Rock Creek Parkway and was sculpted by James Earle Fraser. Each piece stands 17 feet tall and has 36 stars to represent the number of states at the end of the Civil War. On the left are representations of Music and the Harvest, and on the right are Aspiration and Literature. This grouping was also dedicated in 1951.

SITE F4: ARLINGTON MEMORIAL BRIDGE. This bridge, constructed between 1926 and 1932, replaced an older wooden bridge located nearby. It is intended to signify a physical reunification of the North and South after the devastating effects of the Civil War (1861–1865) by connecting the Lincoln Memorial (representing the North) with the Arlington House (representing Robert E. Lee and the South). The large eagles on the sides of the nine pylons were sculpted in bas relief by Carl Paul Jennewein. The bison are 6 feet high and sculpted by Alexander Proctor, who also created the buffalo on the Q Street Bridge over Rock Creek. Near Arlington Cemetery, there are four, 8-foot-high eagles. In the foreground is a floating band stage that was used for concerts until the 1950s.

SITE F5: THE JOHN ERICSSON MONUMENT. This granite piece memorializes the perfection of the screw propeller invented by Swedish-born John Ericsson, who revolutionized navigation. Ericsson's design of the Union ironclad ship the *Monitor* figured in its historic victory over the Confederate *Merrimack* during their encounter at Hampton Roads in March of 1862. Sweden was represented by the crown prince, later known as King Gustavus VI, at the monument's dedication in 1926. Pres. Calvin Coolidge was also in attendance. Ericsson is seated in front with the allegorical figures of Vision, Adventure, and Labor standing against the Norse Tree of Life.

SITE F6: KOREAN WAR VETERANS MEMORIAL. "Freedom is Not Free" is the foremost message of this memorial to the men and women who fought to keep communist North Korea from forcibly reuniting with democratic South Korea. At first, the Korean conflict was an undeclared war, but Pres. Harry Truman committed American troops without Congressional approval on June 25, 1950. Eventually, nearly 1.8 million American troops and units of 22 countries under United Nations auspices would join the conflict. About 54,200 American troops were killed, 103,300 were wounded, and 8,200 were missing in action. Sculptor Frank Gaylord created 19 stainless steel soldiers on patrol through the difficult and wet Korean terrain. Louis Nelson created the etched mural of American soldiers in the black granite wall. The monument was dedicated by Presidents Bill Clinton of the United States and Kim Young Sam of South Korea on July 27, 1995—42 years after the signing of the armistice that ended actual fighting. Technically, at the time of this writing, a state of war still exists between the two Koreas.

SITE F7: FRANKLIN DELANO ROOSEVELT
MEMORIAL.

In this memorial, dedicated to the 32nd president of the United States, water is the central theme in this meandering, 7.5-acre park. Roosevelt became secretary of the Navy, met foreign leaders aboard Navy destroyers while President, regularly visited the spa at Warm Springs, Georgia (where he died in 1945), and generally just loved the water. Sculptors Leonard Baskin, Neil Estern, Robert Graham, Thomas Hardy, and George Segal created four distinct and open areas from the design of Lawrence Halprin, which included nine sculptures and numerous panels of red Dakota granite carved with the words of FDR. The visitor center shows different periods of FDR's life, including a replica of the seldom-seen wheelchair he needed to accommodate his impairment from polio in 1921. The memorial was dedicated on May 2, 1997, by Pres. Bill Clinton, 51 years after Congress introduced and approved a memorial to the longest-serving U.S. president. This Roosevelt served an unprecedented four terms, from 1933 to his death in 1945, spanning both the Great Depression and WW II.

SITES F8 AND F9: JAPANESE PAGODA AND
LANTERN.

These gifts symbolizing Japanese and American friendship were presented by the mayor of Yokohama. Dedicated in 1958, the early-17th-century, nine-tiered granite pagoda depicts four seated Buddhas in bas relief near the base of the structure. The 16th-century granite lantern was dedicated in 1954 on the 100th anniversary of the opening of trade between Japan and the United States by Comm. Matthew Perry. The lantern stands between two of the original Yoshino cherry trees given by Japan to the United States in 1912. The lighting of the lantern signals the beginning of the annual Cherry Blossom Festival held every year during the first week of April since 1934. Actually, Mrs. William Howard Taft planted the first cherry trees in 1907, and the Japanese government added 2,000 more trees five years later. (Note: National Park Service staff tend to move the pagoda and lantern around East Potomac Park. If they are not here, ask a Park Ranger where they've been relocated.)

SITE F10: EAST POTOMAC PARK. This entire island was created as a breakwall by the Army Corps of Engineers in the late 1880s from its dredging operations. The island prevents the seasonal flooding along the Mall that sometimes reached to the foot of Capitol Hill.

SITE F11: THOMAS JEFFERSON MEMORIAL. The memorial to the third president of the United States is a recreation of the rotunda-style design that Jefferson created for his beloved University of Virginia in Charlottesville. The bronze statue of Jefferson stands 19 feet high on a 6-foot-high marble pedestal. Sculptor Rudulph Evans depicts Jefferson in middle age with his long fur-collared coat as he is similarly depicted in the famous Rembrandt Peale portrait. The monument was dedicated on April 13, 1943, by Pres. Franklin D. Roosevelt on the 200th anniversary of Jefferson's birth. The Tidal Basin was created by the Army Corp of Engineers in 1897 to be a flush-basin to clear debris from the nearby Washington Channel during high tides. There are floodgates on either end that raise and lower themselves during high and low tides to keep the nearby channel constantly flushing the harbors. The Tidal Basin was the scene of one of the most celebrated sex scandals in the 1970s. Arkansas Congressman Wilbur Mills, the powerful chairman of the Ways and Means Committee, was arrested along with a local stripper named Fannie Foxe after Foxe was found in the Tidal Basin at 2 a.m. on October 7, 1974. This episode proved to be the end of Mills's congressional influence, and his political career ended on December 10, 1974. The Tidal Basin Beach was on land reclaimed from the Potomac River. A large floating platform was anchored just offshore for diving and general sunbathing.

SITE F12: DISTRICT OF COLUMBIA WAR MEMORIAL. In a grove of magnolias near the Reflecting Pool, a white marble bandstand created by architect Frederick Brooke commemorates the 26,000 Washingtonians who died during WW I. The memorial was dedicated on Armistice Day (Memorial Day) in 1931 by Pres. Herbert Hoover.

SITE F13: COMMODORE JOHN PAUL JONES MEMORIAL. The naval hero of the Revolutionary War is memorialized here in a bronze statue by Charles Henry Niehaus. According to tradition, Jones was the first to raise an American flag on a U.S. naval vessel. He was to have said the fighting words, "Surrender? I have not yet begun to fight!" After his U.S. military service ended, Jones joined the Russian navy as a rear admiral but died in poverty in Paris in 1792. His remains were discovered perfectly preserved in a barrel of rum in a Paris cemetery and re-interred at the U.S. Naval Academy in Annapolis, Maryland. The marble sculpture shows a bas relief of Jones raising the flag on a U.S. warship while dolphins spout water along the pedestal.

SITE F14: CONSTITUTION GARDENS. In 1976, these landscaped gardens and center lake were dedicated to the signers of the Constitution. After 11 years, the United States changed its form of government, which had been based on the inadequate Articles of Confederation, through which each state maintained its own sovereignty except for mutual defense. The nation opted instead for a strong central government under the Constitution of 1789. Along the Constitution Avenue side of the garden is a small wall of rock engraved with the names of each signer in gold. It is a tribute to an enduring document.

MAIN NAVY AND MUNITIONS BUILDINGS. For nearly three-quarters of the 20th century, the military maintained an enormous number of "temporary" buildings on both sides of the Lincoln Memorial and across the Ellipse along Constitution Avenue (buildings on far right). Construction of these buildings began in 1918 during WW I, and 1.8 million square feet of floor space was erected in only six months! The complex housed 14,000 workers in WW I and nearly 30,000 during WW II. The "Main Navy," as it was affectionately known, remained on site until the Vietnam War, and the last structure was finally dismantled in 1971. Finally, L'Enfant's original plan of a Mall uninterrupted from the Lincoln Memorial to the Capitol was achieved. The Organization of American States building is on the far left. This is groundbreaking for additional temporary buildings on what is now the site of Constitution Gardens.

SITE F15: VIETNAM VETERANS MEMORIAL. This memorial, known as "The Wall," is dedicated to the nearly 50,000 servicemen and women who died during the longest war in U.S. history. The triangular black marble monument was designed by Chinese-American Yale student Maya Lin. It was dedicated in 1982. Because the concept was remarkably unlike any traditional monument, a bronze statue featuring three soldiers on patrol was erected just south of the monument in 1984 from a design by Frederick Hart. Later, a flagpole with a U.S. flag was also added nearby. Since its dedication, the Wall has become the most visited monument or museum in Washington, D.C.

SITE F16: VIETNAM WOMEN'S MEMORIAL. On Veterans Day, November 11, 1993, at the dedication of this memorial, Diane Carlson Evans, registered nurse and chair and founder of the Vietnam Women's Memorial Project, said, "We have just unveiled the first monument in the history of the United States of America dedicated . . . to American women who served during wartime." Unveiled by Vice Pres. Al Gore, a Vietnam veteran, the 6-foot, 8-inch multi-figure memorial was sculpted by Glenna Goodacre of Santa Fe, New Mexico. It memorializes the 265,000 military and civilian women who served during the conflict. The memorial depicts a nurse caring for a fallen soldier, while another searches the skies overhead for a helicopter that will lift the soldier to safety.

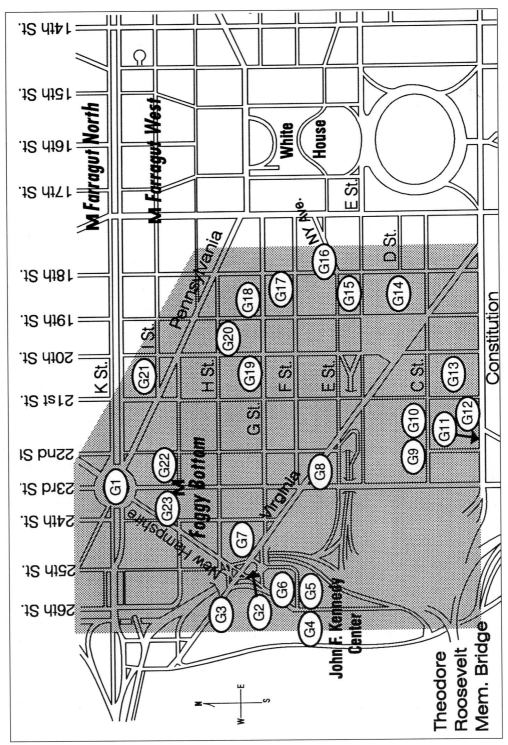

MAP OF FOGGY BOTTOM.

Tour G

FOGGY BOTTOM AND THE
TOWN OF FUNKSTOWN 1765

In 1765, Jacob Funk purchased 130 acres extending, according to Christian Hines, "from about Nineteenth street west to Twenty-fourth street west, and in a northerly direction from the Potomac to about G street north." Funk subdivided his land into 287 lots to sell as speculation, but he didn't quite succeed until L'Enfant included Funkstown in the new Federal City in 1790.

After that, the lots sold well, and Funkstown became a neighborhood of laborers and immigrants. The area remained a lower- to middle-class and poorer neighborhood well into the 19th century.

At Twenty-third Street and Constitution Avenue, the highest point in the area, was Camp Hill, a military post used throughout the War of 1812. Other military posts included the Camp Fry cavalry depot on the site of the National Academy of Sciences and Camp Fuller located near the State Department grounds.

In 1836, the navy built an observatory that shared the riverfront with a cement factory, the Edwards, Way and Company Glass Works built in 1809, and Easby's Wharf and Shipyard. The Washington Gas and Light Company built a large storage facility at New Hampshire and Virginia Avenues in 1856 that lasted for nearly 100 years. Redevelopment in the 20th century eventually removed these structures.

All of that changed when the George Washington University (GWU), originally known as Columbian College in its original charter from Congress in 1821, relocated to Foggy Bottom beginning in 1912. The college had changed its name in 1904. It is the largest landowner in Foggy Bottom today.

Funkstown is now home to the Department of State, along with U.S. Navy facilities, the Kennedy Center, the Watergate Complex, the International Monetary Fund, the World Bank, and Foggy Bottom Metro Station. Of course, its neighborhoods are also wonderful to explore.

SITE G1: WASHINGTON CIRCLE. In the center stands the first statue of George Washington in the Federal City. Congress authorized a statue to George Washington in 1783, but nothing ever came of several proposals until Clark Mills unveiled the statue to Andrew Jackson in Lafayette Square in 1853. Mills designed an elaborate statue with a prominent base featuring all of Washington's generals and scenes from the Revolutionary War. But, due to a lack of funds, only the bronze sculpture of Washington was completed, and it was dedicated in 1860 on this site. Washington's face is taken directly from August Houdon's famous bust of Washington displayed at Mount Vernon. On this site, *c.* 1783, stood Peter's Slashes Plantation, owned by Robert Brent, who was appointed by Thomas Jefferson as the first mayor of the Federal City around 1801. Also, the first race course in Washington operated nearby. Christian Hines remembers the race course located " . . . between F & K and Twenty-first and Twenty-third streets . . . where the western circle [Washington Circle] now is. Horse-racing and cock-fighting . . . were great favorite sports, and they afforded much amusement for the people."

SITE G2: STATUE OF BENITO JUÁREZ AT VIRGINIA AND NEW HAMPSHIRE AVENUE. Succeeding to the presidency of Mexico in 1858 after a rightist coup forced the exile of President Comonfort, Juárez pushed through reforms of the military and significantly reduced the influence of the Catholic church in political affairs. In 1861, after declaring that the immense debt repayment plan was to be suspended, Napolean invaded the country. He forced Juárez to flee the capital city and installed a monarchy. In 1867, Emperor Maximilian was overthrown and executed, and Juárez returned as the legitimate president until his death in 1872. This 12-foot bronze statue, designed by Enrique Alciati, is actually a copy of the original that was executed in 1895 and placed in Juárez's hometown in Oaxaca in southern Mexico. Pres. Lyndon Johnson accepted this as a symbol of friendship with Mexico, and the statue was dedicated here in 1969.

SITE G3: THE WATERGATE COMPLEX AT 2650 VIRGINIA AVENUE. The Watergate Complex was a project spearheaded by the Societa Generale Immobiliare (SGI), an Italian real estate development company. The complex of expensive condominiums, shops, and restaurants was completed in 1971. It was here that on the morning of June 17, 1972, security guard Frank Wills removed tape placed over the door lock on the basement level. This would set off a series of events that led to the capture of five "plumbers" who were burglarizing the Democratic National Committee headquarters on the sixth floor, ostensibly looking for information on the upcoming campaign. Two years later, Pres. Richard Nixon resigned for his role in the ensuing cover-up. A plaque on the sixth floor commemorates this historical event. Across the street at 2601 Virginia Avenue is the former Howard Johnson Motor Hotel (presently known as the Premier Hotel) where the plumbers set up their command post in room 723 to watch for police and Democratic staff members prior to the break-in.

WASHINGTON GAS LIGHT COMPANY (WGLC), 1856. One of the largest and most unsightly enterprises occupied this site for over 100 years. The WGLC and its smokestacks remained a part of the skyline until they were finally dismantled in 1954. Redevelopment of the area, in the form of high-rise apartments and the gentrification of the neighborhoods, soon followed.

SITE G4: THE JOHN F. KENNEDY CENTER FOR THE PERFORMING ARTS. The original location for a national cultural center was to be Constitution Avenue and Seventh Street NW, but the Smithsonian already had plans to construct the National Air and Space Museum on that site. So in 1971, after 12 years of planning, development, fund-raising, and construction (from a design by Edward Durrell Stone), the cultural center was finally dedicated and named as a memorial to the assassinated 35th President of the United States. Legend has it that the mysterious "Deep Throat" met with Woodward and Bernstein in the underground parking garage during their investigation of the Watergate break-in. Here you can visit the Hall of States, the Grand Foyer, and the Hall of Nations. There is also a great view from the veranda. Nearby, just south of the Kennedy Center, is Braddock's Landing. According to legend, this was where Gen. Edward Braddock stepped ashore with his aide, Lt. Col. George Washington, on his way to fight the French and Indians at Fort Duquesne, near Pittsburgh, in 1755.

CHRISTIAN HEURICH BREWERY: 1892–1961. On this site, a brewery operated by German immigrant Christian Heurich produced 100,000 barrels of Senate Beer during its heyday. During Prohibition, the brewery served as an ice-making plant. Heurich managed the facility until he died in 1945 at the age of 102. Beer was no longer made here after 1956 or so, and the large building was finally condemned by the city in 1961. The Arena Stage Company made it their home in 1955 and remained there until condemnation forced them to move to their own building at Sixth and M Streets SW. The brewery was razed in 1966 for the construction of the John F. Kennedy Center for the Performing Arts.

SITE G5: DON QUIXOTE DE LA MANCHA. This wonderful artistic rendering of the famous character from the novel by Miguel de Cervantes was created by sculptor Antonio Teno of Madrid for the U.S. Bicentennial in 1976. King Juan Carlos of Spain dedicated the bronze statue as a gift from the Cultural Institute of Spain in June 1976.

SITE G6: ROYAL EMBASSY OF SAUDI ARABIA AT 601 NEW HAMPSHIRE AVENUE. The embassy and chancery offices relocated to this former insurance office building in 1983. On occasion, you can see the green and white national flag of Saudi Arabia flying above the building during the day. Green is thought to have been the color of the Prophet Mohammad's turban and has therefore been an important symbol in the Islam religion. The current flag dates to 1938 and is the traditional Wahabi banner belonging to Abd al-Aziz ibn Saud, leader of the Wahabis and the founder and namesake of Saudi Arabia. The flag is the only one in the world with an inscription as its design. The Shahada (or Word of Unity of Islam) states the following: "There is no god but Allah and Muhammad is the Prophet of Allah." The sword is a Wahabi symbol for militancy. The date palm (representing the key agricultural product) over two crossed scimitars is the royal arms, representing the royal family of Saudi Arabia. *Open to the public. Call the information office at (202)944-5949 for reservations Monday through Friday 9 a.m. to 5 p.m.*

SITE G7: COLUMBIA PLAZA APARTMENTS AT 2400 VIRGINIA AVENUE. This was part of the urban renewal project envisioned for the Foggy Bottom area after the dismantling of some large and unsightly industrial buildings. This complex of condominiums and apartments was built in 1962. According to writer Jim Hougan in his book *Secret Agenda*, these apartments were under surveillance by the CIA to uncover a prostitution ring being run out of the chairman's office at the Democratic National Committee. Hougan claims that this was the real story behind the break-in at the Watergate. Hougan's theory has yet to be proven.

SITE G8: WORLD HEALTH ORGANIZATION AT 525 23RD STREET. The World Health Organization (WHO) was organized by the United Nations in 1948 in order to improve health and welfare throughout the world. Located here is the Pan American Health Organization, responsible for the health concerns of the United States, Canada, and Central and South America. The unusual architecture of this curved headquarters building with a round council chamber fits rather well within the 1-acre triangular site. Designed by architect Roman Fresnedo Siri, this building was constructed in 1961. Four fountains were to be added in the plaza area, but they were never built. The founding nations are represented by their distinctive bronze national coat-of-arms along the lower exterior of the building. Each one, designed by sculptor Michael Lantz of the United States, is 2.5 feet in diameter.

SITE G9: THE DEPARTMENT OF STATE. Originally in 1800, the State Department was housed in a separate building on the northeast side of the White House grounds until 1820 when a brick building was constructed on the site. The State Department moved to the almost completed Old Executive Office Building next to the White House in 1866. It then moved to these new buildings at Foggy Bottom created by architect Alfred B. Mullett in 1947. Just inside the main entrance are the approximately 190 flags representing every country diplomatically recognized by the United States. When the secretary is onsite, the official flag is flown at this entrance. It is a dark-blue flag featuring a white circle in the center. Inside this center is a full-color representation of the Great Seal of the United States, which was introduced in 1782 and last modernized in 1885. Additionally, there is a white flag in each corner. This design dates back to a presidential standard introduced for the U.S. military in 1916. In 1945, the current presidential flag was introduced and its predecessor (this design) was downgraded to the flag of the secretary of state.

SITE G10: THE NAVAL OBSERVATORY, 1844. The idea for a coordinated body to gather astronomical observations for use in nautical astronomy began with William Lambert in 1809. It wasn't until 1830 that a depot was created for the storage of charts and instruments for the U.S. Navy. The first observatory was built at personal expense by Lt. Charles Wilkes, the superintendent of the depot. Finally, in 1844, the first Naval Observatory was established on this site under Congressional authority and still stands as part of the Navy Medical Command. The observatory moved to Wisconsin Avenue and Thirty-fourth Street NW in 1893, a site which also became the home of the Vice President of the United States in 1977. On this site, L'Enfant placed Camp Hill, an early military encampment, to take advantage of the hill's unusual height. During the War of 1812 and up until the Naval Observatory was built, this site was known as Camp Hill.

SITE G11: NATIONAL ACADEMY OF SCIENCES AT 2101 CONSTITUTION AVENUE NW. Before 1920, the National Academy of Sciences had their offices at the Smithsonian Institution. This Beaux Arts-style building was designed by architect Bertram C. Goodhue, but the sculpture and exterior detail were created by sculptor Lee Lawrie. The large, 8-foot-wide bronze bas relief sculptures between the windows depict the progress of science through the modern era. The large bronze doors show eight episodes of the history of science, from Aristotle to Louis Pasteur. The Albert Einstein Memorial, just in front of the Academy, facing Constitution Avenue, is a 21-foot-high black granite sculpture of the famed scientist created by sculptor Robert Berks. It was dedicated here in 1979. Einstein holds a copy of his theory of relativity in his right hand. *Open to the public Monday through Friday 9 a.m. to 5 p.m.*

SITE G13: FEDERAL RESERVE BOARD AT CONSTITUTION AVENUE AND 20TH STREET NW. The system of regional reserve banks is overseen by a board of governors known collectively as the Federal Reserve Board. Each member is appointed by the President and confirmed by the Senate. Together, they administer the Federal Reserve Act of 1913 and serve as a central bank. One of their key functions is the setting of interest rates for its member banks. For its headquarters, architect Paul Cret created a simple, Classical-style building of Georgian marble, whose only embellishments are the bas relief carvings over the C Street main entrance of a 6-foot-high eagle by Sidney Waugh. The two female figures represent America (right) and the Federal Reserve Board (left). Each measures about 10 feet tall and both were sculpted by John Gregory. The building was dedicated in 1937.

SITE G14: DEPARTMENT OF THE INTERIOR AT C STREET BETWEEN EIGHTEENTH AND NINETEENTH STREETS NW. As the old joke goes, the Department of the Interior is responsible for everything outside. The department got its start in 1849 under Pres. James K. Polk (who, incidentally, has been the only Speaker of the House to become President) to manage the sale of public lands for homesteads. Its responsibilities have grown beyond the original functions to include the National Park Service, the Bureau of Mines, the Bureau of Indian Affairs, the U.S. Geological Survey, and more. The building itself was designed by Washington architect Waddy B. Wood and constructed in 1935-36, its only ornamentation consisting of the seals of the 13 original colonies along the C Street entrance. However, in the courtyard are four very well-received bronze statues, including *Negro and Child* designed by Maurice Glickman in 1934 and *Abe Lincoln, Rail Joiner,* designed by Louis Slobodkin in 1940. Other murals and artwork along the corridors date from the renaissance period of the Works Progress Administration of the Depression era.

SITE G15: RAWLINS PARK AT EIGHTEENTH AND E STREETS NW. Maj. Gen. John A. Rawlins was aide-de-camp to Ulysses S. Grant throughout the Civil War and became his secretary of war after Grant was elected the 18th President of the United States. Due to the tuberculosis he had contracted two years earlier, Rawlins died within five months of his 1869 appointment. This simple bronze statue was erected here in 1874 from a design by sculptor Joseph A. Bailey. It is said that it was cast from Confederate cannons captured during the war.

SITE G16: OCTAGON HOUSE AT NEW YORK AVENUE AND EIGHTEENTH STREET NW.
Though it really only has six sides, each side has an angle, which explains why it is called an octagon house. This Federal-style brick house was built *c.* 1800 by Col. John Tayloe, who was a personal friend of George Washington and a wealthy planter himself. The Octagon House became an important social center of early Washington. When the British burned the nearby White House in 1814, they bypassed the Octagon House because the house may have flown the French flag courtesy of the tenant, the ambassador of France. After the British retreated, Pres. James Madison returned and made the Octagon House the temporary White House for a few months. In fact, it was on the second floor that the Treaty of Ghent was signed, ending the war with Great Britain on February 4, 1815. During the Civil War, the house was confiscated by the government and used as a military hospital. After the war, it became a Catholic school and government offices. In 1899, the American Institute of Architects (AIA) bought the house and restored it as offices and museum. The AIA headquarters wraps around the Octagon House from behind. *Open to the public 10 a.m. to 4 p.m. daily; closed on Monday. Admission fee.* *(202)538-3105.*

SITE G17: JOHN MARSHALL HOUSE AT 1801 F STREET NW. This red brick townhouse, built in 1825, was a rooming house for most of its early existence. It served as the home of many important figures, including Supreme Court Chief Justice John Marshall, Presidents James Madison, James Monroe, and Martin Van Buren, and Civil War general George McLellan.

SITE G18: INTERNATIONAL MONETARY FUND (IMF) AT 700 NINETEENTH STREET NW.
The IMF was created as an independent agency of the United Nations to "promote international monetary cooperation and currency stabilization" and to also promote expansion of international trade. Their new headquarters was built in 1973 and features an immense covered courtyard inside. The first Baptist Congregation worshipped here until 1833 when the First Colored Baptist Church of the City of Washington took over the congregation until 1871. From that time, the Nineteenth Street Baptist Church stood here until 1974, according to a plaque on the site.

SITE G19: THE GEORGE WASHINGTON UNIVERSITY AT THE CORNER OF G AND TWENTIETH STREETS NW. Originally named Columbian College at its founding in 1819, this university was intended as a theological training center for a group of Washington Baptists. By Act of Congress in 1821,"The Columbian College in the District of Columbia" was incorporated. Its first commencement in 1824 was attended by Pres. James Monroe and General Marquis de Lafayette. In 1873, the name was changed to Columbian University, but financial difficulties ensued. Philanthropist W.W. Corcoran provided the university with its first endowment, thereby ensuring its success. In 1904, the Baptist Convention changed the school's name to George Washington University to honor the first President.

SITE G20: UNION METHODIST EPISCOPAL CHURCH AT H AND TWENTIETH STREETS NW. The original church was founded in 1846 on the southeast corner of Nineteenth and H Streets NW and moved to this location in 1910. The church merged with the Concordia Church at 1920 G Street in 1985. Now, this building is leased to George Washington University.

SITE G21: THE MONROE HOUSE (CALDWELL HOUSE) AT 2017 I STREET NW. This brick, federal-style house was built in 1802 by Timothy Caldwell. After leaving the White House in 1817, Pres. James Monroe briefly moved into this house. The house later served as the British Legation and the home of other diplomats. The Arts Club of Washington has been located here since 1916.

SITE G22: THE GEORGE WASHINGTON UNIVERSITY HOSPITAL AT 901 TWENTY-THIRD STREET NW. On March 30, 1981, Pres. Ronald Reagan, only ten weeks into his first term, was shot after giving a speech at the Washington Hilton Hotel. He was rushed here where emergency surgery saved his life. Reagan recovered and went on to sign the "Brady Bill." Named for James Brady, who was also wounded at the site, the bill requires a seven-day waiting period for the purchase of a handgun.

NATIONAL MEDICAL COLLEGE.

The *National Medical College of the Columbian University*, on H st., between 13th and 14th sts. N. W., was founded in 1824. The building was the gift of W. W. Corcoran, 1864, cost $40,000, was originally intended for a mechanics' library and lectures, contains two *lecture rooms*, with *ante rooms*, *chemical laboratory*, and *dissecting room*. In winter the janitor will admit visitors. The *Dispensary* is open daily, except Sunday, from 1 to 3 p. m.. to the poor.

SITE G23: ST. MARY'S EPISCOPAL CHURCH AT 728 TWENTY-THIRD STREET. In the late 19th century, Foggy Bottom was home to mostly lower-middle-class laborers, although there were some pockets of prosperity. The Civil War brought many African-American residents to Foggy Bottom, but in order to worship they had to walk to St. John's Church in Lafayette Square and the Church of the Epiphany at Thirteenth and G Streets. Segregation forced these members to worship in the balconies, and they could take Communion only after the white members had done so. Wishing to correct the problem, white congregation members donated a site for a separate church that was designed by James Renwick. This present church (the original church operated in a converted Civil War barracks on this site beginning in 1867) was consecrated in 1886 as St. Mary's Chapel for Colored People. It was the first African-American Episcopal church in Washington, D.C., and has been a community place of worship ever since. Visit the Herbert Files garden and the Tiffany window dedicated to Lincoln's secretary of war, Edwin Stanton. St. Mary's was named a national historic landmark in 1972.

Selective Bibliography

American Guide Series. *Washington: City and Capital*. Writers Project, Works Progress Administration, General Printing Office, 1937.

American Institute of Architects. *A Guide to the Architecture of Washington, DC*. Third Edition, McGraw-Hill Book Company, 1994.

Arnebeck, Bob. *Through a Fiery Trial: Building Washington 1790–1800*. Madison Books, 1991.

Beale, Marie. *Decatur House and Its Inhabitants*. National Trust for Historic Preservation, 1954.

Cable, Mary. *Avenue of the Presidents*. Houghton Mifflin, 1969.

Evelyn, Douglas E., and Paul Dickson. *On This Spot: Pinpointing the Past in Washington, DC*. On This Spot Productions, Maryland, 1992.

Executive Office of the President. *The Old Executive Office Building: A Victorian Masterpiece*. Office of Administration, Government Printing Office, 1984.

Fitzpatrick, Sandra, and Maria R. Goodwin. *The Guide to Black Washington*. Hippocrene Books, Inc., 1993.

Goode, James M. *Outdoor Sculpture of Washington, DC*. Smithsonian Institute Press, 1979.

Goode, James M. *Capital Losses: A Cultural History of Washington's Destroyed Buildings*. Smithsonian Institute Press, 1979.

Hall, Clayton Colman, ed. *Narratives of Early Maryland*. Charles Scribner's Sons, 1910.

Hines, Christian. *Early Recollections of Washington City*. Junior League, reprint 1981.

Junior League. *The City of Washington Illustrated*. Alfred A. Knopf, 1985.

Katz, D. Mark. *Witness to an Era: The Life and Photographs of Alexander Gardner*. Rutledge Hill Press, 1991.

Leech, Margaret. *Reveille in Washington*. New York, 1941.

Lord, Walter. *The Dawn's Early Light*. W.W. Norton & Co., 1972.

Reed, Robert. *Old Washington, DC in Early Photographs: 1846–1932*. Dover Publications, 1980.

Schwartz, Nancy B. *Historic American Buildings Survey: District of Columbia Catalog*. University Press of Virginia, 1974.

Taylor, Benjamin Ogle. *Our Neighbors on LaFayette Square*. Junior League, reprint 1981.

White House Historical Association. *The White House*. Government Printing Office, 1994.

Washburn, Wilcomb E. *The Cosmos Club of Washington: A Centennial History 1878–1978*. The Cosmos Club, 1978.

Photo Credits:

All images are courtesy of the Washingtoniana Division, D.C. Public Library except for the following: Site A5: Statue of Freedom, courtesy of Architect of the U.S. Capitol; Site A6: Senator Russell, courtesy of United States Senate Historical Office; Site A7: Senator Dirksen, courtesy of United States Senate Historical Office; Site A8: Senator Hart, courtesy of United States Senate Historical Office; Site A9: Sewall-Belmont House by the author; Site A10: Bayly House by the author; Site A12: Folger Shakespeare Theatre by the author, Grant's Row, courtesy of the Historical Society of Washington, D.C.; Site A13: Frederick Douglass Home and Museum by the author, Frederick Douglass, copyright the *Washington Post* reprinted by permission of the Washington D.C. Public Library; Site A16: St. Mark's Church by the author; Site A17: painting of John Adams, courtesy of the Architect of the U.S. Capitol; Site A21: Cannon, courtesy of the Architect of the U.S. Capitol; Site A22: Longworth, courtesy of the Architect of the U.S. Capitol; Site A23: Cong. Rayburn, courtesy of the Architect of the U.S. Capitol; Site A25: Botanic Garden by the author; Site A26: James Garfield, courtesy of Architect of the U.S. Capitol; Site A30: Capitol Grotto by the author; Site A31: Sen. Taft, courtesy of the Architect of the U.S. Capitol; Site B1: Chinese Arch by the author; Site B3: McLellan, courtesy of Albert Eisenberg; Site B4: Small Jewish Museum by the author; Site B5: Pension Building in author's collection; Site B8: Lincoln Statue by the author; Site B10: Blackstone Statue by the author; Site B15: Federal Trade Commission Building by the author; Site B20: Hancock Memorial by the author; Site B22: Gardner's Studio, courtesy of Prints and Photographs Division, Library of Congress; Site B24: Clara Barton's Boarding House by the author; Site B27: Patent Office in author's collection; Site B28: Metropolitan Theater, copyright the *Washington Post* reprinted by permission of the Washington D.C. Public Library; Site C4: Hirshhorn Museum by the author; Site C5: Armory Square Hospital, courtesy of Al Eisenberg; Site C6: Hubert Humphrey, courtesy of United States Senate Historical Office; Site C10: National Archives by the author; Site C11: Natural History Building by the author; Site C13: Washington Monument in author's collection; Site C14: Jefferson's Pier by the author; Site C15: Holocaust Museum by the author; Site C16: plate of Bureau of Printing and Engraving in author's collection; Site C18: Sackler Gallery by the author; Site C19: Museum of African Art by the author; Site C20: Baird statue by the author; Site C21: Downing Urn by the author; Site D2: Navy Urn by the author; Site D4: painting of Lafayette, courtesy of the Architect of the U.S. Capitol; Site D6: the Belasco Theater, copyright the *Washington Post* reprinted by permission of the Washington D.C. Public Library; Site D25: painting of Abraham Lincoln, courtesy of the Architect of the U.S. Capitol, U.S. Grant, courtesy of Al Eisenberg; Site E3: Zero Milestone by the author; Site E4: National Christmas Tree by the author; Site E6: Red Cross building by the author; Site E8: Van Ness Carriage House by the author; Site E10: Bulfinch Gatehouse by the author; Site E13: Settler's Stone by the author; Site E14: Boy Scout Memorial by the author; Site E16: Pershing statue by the author; Site E17: Sherman, courtesy of Al Eisenberg; Site E24: Riggs Bank by the author, Lincoln Monument under construction in author's collection; Site F2: Arts of War by the author; Site F3: Arts of Peace by the author; Site F6: Korean War Memorial by the author; Site F8: Japanese Pagoda by the author; Site F9: Japanese Lantern by the author; Site F12: DC War Memorial by the author; Site F13: painting of John Paul Jones, courtesy of the Architect of the U.S. Capitol; Site F15: Vietnam Memorial by the author, Vietnam Women's Memorial by the author; Site G2: Juarez statue by the author; Site G3: Watergate by the author; Site G4: Heurich Brewery, courtesy of the Historical Society of Washington D.C.; Site G5: Don Quixote statue by the author; Site G6: of Saudi Arabia Embassy by the author; Site G7: Columbia Plaza Apartments by the author; Site G8: World Health Organization by the author; Site G13: Federal Reserve in author's collection; Site G14: Dept. of Interior by the author; Site G17: Marshall House by the author, painting of John Marshall, courtesy of Architect of the U.S. Capitol; Site G18: Int'l Monetary Fund building by the author; Site G20: Union Methodist Church by the author; Site G21: Monroe House by the author; Site G23: St. Mary:s Church by the author.

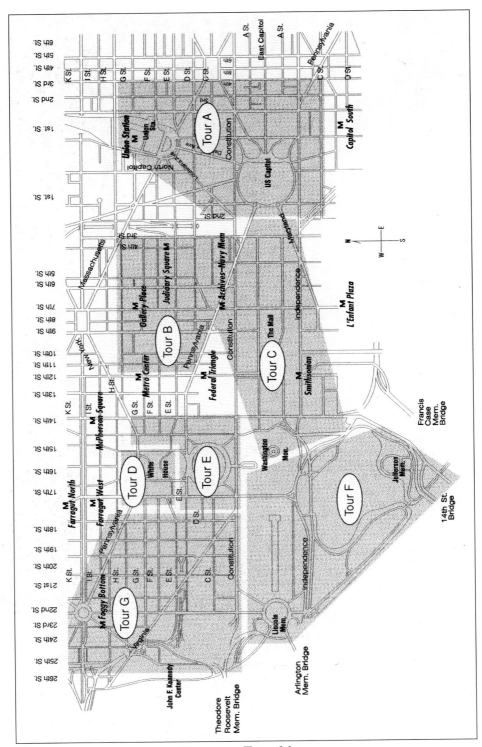

COMPLETE TOUR MAP.